CONTENTS

KU-373-073

PART FOUR:
FORM, STRUCTURE AND LANGUAGE

PART FIVE:
COMPARING POEMS IN THE CLUSTER

PART SIX:
APPROACHING 'UNSEEN' POEMS

PART SEVEN:
PROGRESS BOOSTER ⭐

PART EIGHT:
FURTHER STUDY AND ANSWERS

PREPARING FOR ASSESSMENT

HOW WILL I BE ASSESSED ON MY WORK ON *LOVE AND RELATIONSHIPS?*

When studying the cluster, your work will be examined through these three Assessment Objectives:

Assessment Objectives	Wording	Worth thinking about ...
AO1	Read, understand and respond to texts. Students should be able to: • maintain a critical style and develop an informed personal response • use textual references, including quotations, to support and illustrate interpretations.	• How well do I know what happens, what people say, do, etc. in each poem? • What do *I* think about the key ideas in the poems? • How can I support my viewpoint in a really convincing way? • What are the best quotations to use and when should I use them?
AO2	Analyse the language, form and structure used by a writer to create meanings and effects, using relevant subject terminology where appropriate.	• What specific things do the poets 'do'? What choices has each poet made? (Why this particular word, phrase or image here? Why does this change occur at this point?) • What effects do these choices create – optimism, pessimism, ambiguity?
AO3 *	Show understanding of the relationships between texts and the contexts in which they were written.	• What can I learn about society from the poems? (What do they tell me about stereotypes and prejudice, for example?) • What was/is society like for the poets? Can I see it reflected in their poems?

*AO3 is only assessed in relation to the cluster, and not in relation to the 'Unseen' part of the exam (see **Part Six: Approaching 'unseen' poems**).

In other parts of your English Literature GCSE a fourth Assessment Objective, **AO4**, which is related to spelling, punctuation and grammar, is also assessed. While you will not gain any marks for AO4 in your poetry examination, it is still important to ensure that you write accurately and clearly, in order to get your points across to the examiner in the best possible way.

Look out for the Assessment Objective labels throughout your York Notes Study Guide – these will help to focus your study and revision!

The text used in this Study Guide is *Past and Present: Poetry Anthology* (AQA, 2015).

HOW TO USE YOUR YORK NOTES STUDY GUIDE

In this York Notes Study Guide you will find the text of every poem in the cluster, fully annotated, plus over 20 pages of detailed analysis of themes, contexts, structure, form and language. There are special sections on comparing poems and the 'unseen' part of your exam, three sample practice papers, and annotated sample answers at three different levels.

So how will these Notes help you study and revise? Here are some suggestions:

- **A step-by-step study and revision guide** – work through the poems in Part Two to help you study them, then use the analysis sections to focus your learning. Finally, hone your exams skills and practise for the exam.
- **A 'dip-in' support** – know the cluster quite well already but want to check your understanding and practise your skills? Look for the section you think you need most help with, and go for it!
- **A revision guide before your exam** – use Parts Two to Four to check your knowledge, then work through Parts Five to Eight as you revise for your exam.

Short and long questions to test your knowledge and understanding

Every poem annotated with lots of useful ideas and interpretations

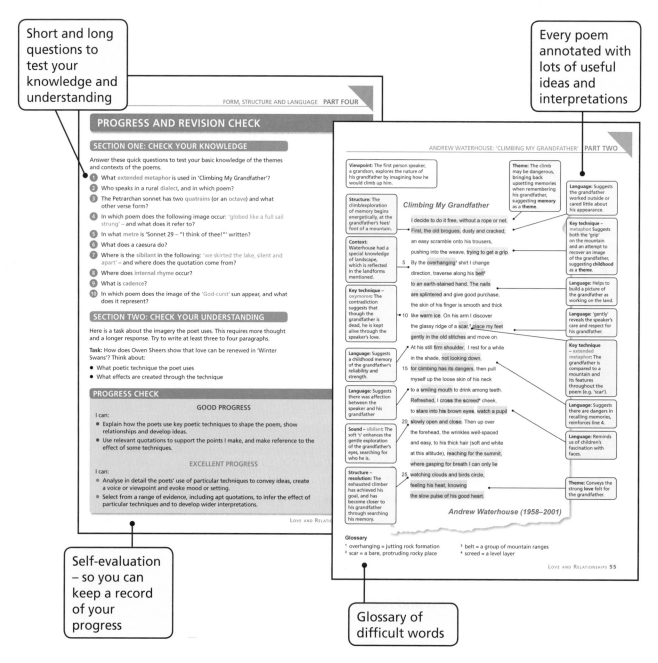

Self-evaluation – so you can keep a record of your progress

Glossary of difficult words

PART TWO: EXPLORING THE POEMS

HOW TO READ AND STUDY A POEM

When you read and study a poem, or a set of poems, there are a number of key areas you will need to explore. These will ensure you enjoy your reading and study, and equally importantly, engage with the poem so that you can respond intelligently and thoughtfully.

KEY ASPECTS TO CONSIDER

As with any text, the secret to exploring the poem on the page in front of you is to consider its ingredients: the particular elements that create meaning or impact on you as a reader. These will include:

1 What the **narrative** of the poem is – its story, or the experience it describes

For example, does the poem describe something particular that happens? Is it a personal story or a public one? What actually happens? (Sometimes poems don't seem to tell a story at all, but all poems are about *something*, however small or apparently insignificant.)

2 The **voice** (or voices) and **viewpoint**

For example, is the poem told in the first person, and is the voice intimate or distant? Who does it address?

3 The **'message'** and/or **theme** of the poem – its concerns

For example, what is the main idea running through the poem? Are there other, related ideas?

4 The poem's distinctive **language features**, or **poetic techniques** used by the poet

What method or skills does the poet use to create effects? For example poets often use enjambment because it carries the thought on from one line to another.

5 The poem's **structure** and **organisation**

For example, is the poem written in a particular form, such as a sonnet or a monologue? Are the verses regular (with the same number of lines in a verse)? Is there a rhyme scheme?

6 The **openings** and **endings**

For example, does it provide a resolution to a problem? Or does the reader feel something is unresolved? Does the ending return to the beginning to create a circular effect? Does it change the reader's understanding of the poem?

7 **Patterns** of **sound** and **rhythm**

For example, what sounds are created through the repetition of letters, such as beginning letters in alliteration, or vowels in assonance? What is the movement of the poem like? For example, is it bouncy comic poem, a slow lament or a sad song? Does the pace change?

8 **Contexts** and **settings**

For example, what influenced the poet? Do you know the historical period in which the poem was written? Is a period referred to or expressed in the poem, such as the speaker recalling a memory from the past? Can you tell when or where the poem was set?

TOP TIP **A01**

Always read a poem at least twice before you begin writing about it. On your first reading you are likely to get a general impression of the poem's tone and what it is about. On your second reading try to focus on the rhythm and language choice. You should find the meaning becomes clearer you start to notice the poet's techniques and their effects.

When We Two Parted

Form: Four octaves and regular rhyme reinforce the **repetition**.

Structure: Two stressed syllables **repeated** in every line, reminiscent of chant/ **lament**.

Language: Suggests decline and death, accentuating the idea that the relationship is at an end.

Theme – separation: The lover's 'kiss' is distant.

Language – vocabulary choice: 'dew' reinforces the images of 'tears' and 'Sorrow', stanza one.

Language: Appeals to the sense of touch. Also suggests panic, relating to the speaker's fear of the future.

Key technique – **foreshadowing:** See lines 7–8.

Key technique: The lover's name is a **metaphor** for the bell rung at funerals, emphasising the death of love.

When we two parted

In silence and **tears**,

Half broken-hearted

To sever for years,

5   Pale grew thy cheek and cold,

Colder thy kiss;

Truly that hour foretold

Sorrow to this.

The dew of the morning

10   Sunk chill on my brow –

It felt like the warning

Of what I feel now.

Thy vows are all broken,

And light is thy fame;

15   I hear thy name spoken,

And share in its shame.

They name thee before me,

A knell in mine ear;

A shudder comes o'er me –

20   Why wert thou so dear?

They know not I knew thee,

Theme – separation: Strong opening suggests the key theme.

Theme – separation: 'half' implies only the speaker's heart is broken.

Context – Romanticism: Concerned with intense feelings, as in the pain of parting.

Language: Appeals to the sense of touch. Suggests sickness and death and links to 'Pale'.

Key technique – **foreshadowing:** The lovers' parting (stanza one) suggested 'Sorrow' and 'shame' would follow (stanza two).

Viewpoint: First person (speaker) addresses second person (lover); emphasises an intimate relationship.

Key technique – irony: Those who gossip about the lover in front of the speaker are unaware she was the speaker's lover.

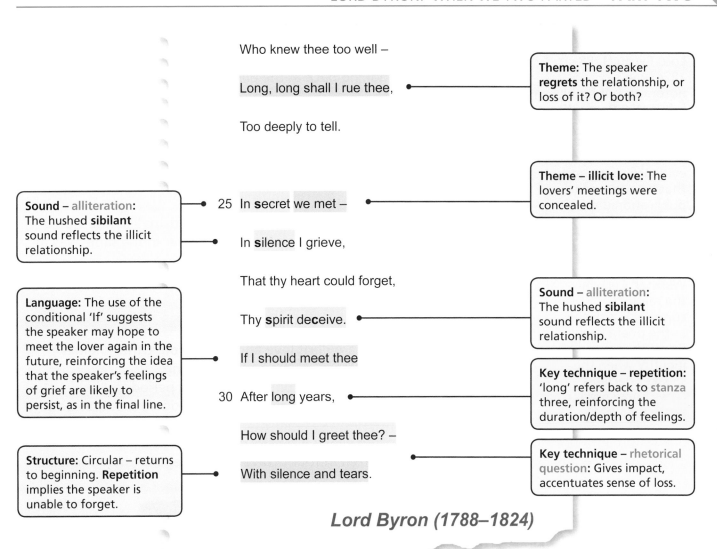

Who knew thee too well –

Long, long shall I rue thee,

Too deeply to tell.

25 In **s**ecret we met –

In **s**ilence I grieve,

That thy heart could forget,

Thy **s**pirit de**c**eive.

If I should meet thee

30 After long years,

How should I greet thee? –

With silence and tears.

Lord Byron (1788–1824)

Theme: The speaker **regrets** the relationship, or loss of it? Or both?

Theme – illicit love: The lovers' meetings were concealed.

Sound – alliteration: The hushed **sibilant** sound reflects the illicit relationship.

Sound – alliteration: The hushed **sibilant** sound reflects the illicit relationship.

Language: The use of the conditional 'If' suggests the speaker may hope to meet the lover again in the future, reinforcing the idea that the speaker's feelings of grief are likely to persist, as in the final line.

Key technique – repetition: 'long' refers back to stanza three, reinforcing the duration/depth of feelings.

Structure: Circular – returns to beginning. **Repetition** implies the speaker is unable to forget.

Key technique – rhetorical question: Gives impact, accentuates sense of loss.

Structure: Time shifts – past (stanza one), past/present (2), present (3), future (4) – suggest the speaker's feelings will last forever.

KEY CONTEXT **A03**

Lord Byron (1788–1824) was a notorious but highly influential **Romantic** poet, who died young of fever in Greece. There is evidence to suggest that he altered the publication date of 'When We Two Parted' to protect Lady Frances Wedderburn Webster. Certainly the reader's curiosity is aroused, as the poem keeps secret the lover's identity when the speaker declares, 'They know not I knew thee' (21).

SUMMARY

- The speaker is looking back at the end of an illicit relationship.
- He recalls the sorrow of the parting, the coldness of the lover and the sense of foreboding he felt.
- Now that the lover has become the object of gossip, the speaker shares a sense of guilt, albeit secretly.
- He can no longer understand why the lover was important to him, and regrets the affair.
- He silently mourns her faithlessness, and he anticipates that should they meet again years later he would receive her in the same way as when they parted.

KEY ASPECTS OF THE POEM

A The main themes are **illicit love** and **separation**. Other themes include, **unfaithfulness**, **regret** and **foreboding**.

B The poem is a lyric poem from the Romantic period.

C The poem is told in the **first person** and the poem is addressed to the ex-lover.

D The images often evoke **intensity of feeling**.

E The poem is written in four octaves with a regular rhyme scheme.

TOP TIP: WRITING ABOUT LINKED THEMES **A02**

Remember that the themes in the poem are closely related. For example, the illicit nature of the love expressed in the poem emphasises secrecy. This is related to the theme of foreboding – a fear not only of discovery and 'shame' (16) but also of betrayal.

KEY SETTING: SHIFTS IN TIME   **A01**

Byron creates no specific setting in the poem other than the time of day when the lovers parted, which was early morning when the 'dew' (9) had fallen. **Stanzas** one and two focus on the recollection of this parting – an unidentified moment. There is then a shift in time in stanza two. We are brought forward into the poem's present when the speaker realises that the loved one has become the object of rumour: 'They name thee before me' (17). Here, we can only imagine a group of people in conversation without a specific sense of place. Finally, we are taken into the future when the speaker imagines what might happen if he and his lover ever 'should meet' (29) again. This lack of setting heightens the secrecy, an important theme in the poem. It also stresses intensity of feeling (a feature of Romantic poetry) – the reader, who has limited information about the external world, must focus on the inner feelings of the speaker.

AIMING HIGH: A KEY REPETITION   ★

The poem opens as the speaker recalls parting from his lover in 'silence and tears' (2). The image is repeated at the end of the poem, so that even 'After long years' (30) the speaker supposes that his feelings would not have altered. The effect that Byron creates by using repetition is to drive home the depth of feeling of loss. However, by placing the words 'silence and tears' (2, 32) at the beginning of the poem and at the end, Byron also creates a circular effect. The reader is returned to the beginning of the poem and the speaker's memory of 'when we two parted' (1) – to the title as well as the first line of the poem. So we are left with the impression that the speaker may never be free of the intense emotional memory and nature of the parting.

KEY TECHNIQUE: A GRIM IRONY   **A02**

In the third stanza Byron creates a grim and complex **irony**. The lover's name is mentioned (presumably at a social gathering). Those present are not aware that the named woman was the speaker's lover, 'They know not I knew thee' (21), and are unaware that he knew her 'too well' (22). And there is further irony in the speaker knowing her 'too well' (22) or being too close. He has learnt to his sorrow that despite their closeness she has still 'broken' her 'vows' (13) and physically separated him from her.

KEY LANGUAGE: IMAGERY OF PAIN   **A02**

Much of the imagery Byron creates is associated with pain: of separation, of lovesickness and grief. A verb such as 'sever' (4) depicts a brutal separation. It also has associations with cutting and wounding, while 'Half broken-hearted' (3) implies it is only one heart that is broken: the speaker's. Images of the lover's 'pale' 'cold' 'cheek' (5) suggest loss of passion. The 'chill' on the speaker's 'brow' (10) suggests sickness, or lovesickness. In stanza three the lover's name sounds 'a knell' (18), which causes the speaker to 'shudder' (19). Both these words are reminiscent of the bell rung at funerals; a **metaphor** for the love that has died. The images reinforce the speaker's pain and act as a commentary on human nature and its capacity to hurt others.

TOP TIP   **A02**

Notice how the words 'hour foretold' (7) in stanza one and 'warning' (11) in stanza two **foreshadow** the shame the speaker shares with the lover who has become the subject of rumour.

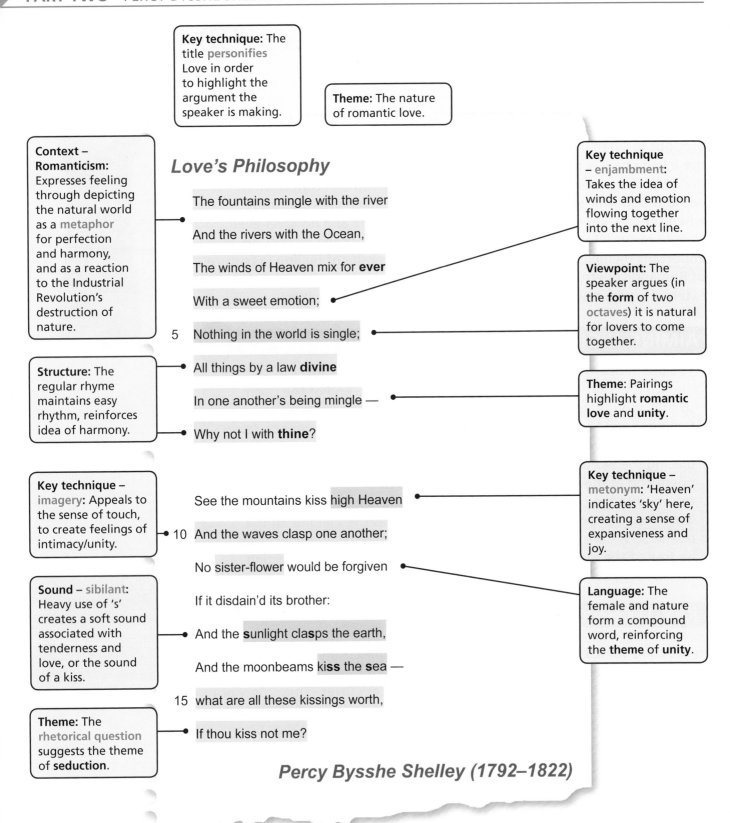

Key technique: The title **personifies** Love in order to highlight the argument the speaker is making.

Theme: The nature of romantic love.

Context – Romanticism: Expresses feeling through depicting the natural world as a **metaphor** for perfection and harmony, and as a reaction to the Industrial Revolution's destruction of nature.

Structure: The regular rhyme maintains easy rhythm, reinforces idea of harmony.

Key technique – imagery: Appeals to the sense of touch, to create feelings of intimacy/unity.

Sound – sibilant: Heavy use of 's' creates a soft sound associated with tenderness and love, or the sound of a kiss.

Theme: The **rhetorical question** suggests the theme of **seduction**.

Key technique – enjambment: Takes the idea of winds and emotion flowing together into the next line.

Viewpoint: The speaker argues (in the **form** of two **octaves**) it is natural for lovers to come together.

Theme: Pairings highlight **romantic love** and **unity**.

Key technique – metonym: 'Heaven' indicates 'sky' here, creating a sense of expansiveness and joy.

Language: The female and nature form a compound word, reinforcing the **theme** of **unity**.

Love's Philosophy

The fountains mingle with the river

And the rivers with the Ocean,

The winds of Heaven mix for **ever**

With a sweet emotion;

5 Nothing in the world is single;

All things by a law **divine**

In one another's being mingle —

Why not I with **thine**?

See the mountains kiss high Heaven

10 And the waves clasp one another;

No sister-flower would be forgiven

If it disdain'd its brother:

And the **s**unlight cla**s**ps the earth,

And the moonbeams ki**ss** the **s**ea —

15 what are all these kissings worth,

If thou kiss not me?

Percy Bysshe Shelley (1792–1822)

Structure: Lines 5, 6 (first octave) present the speaker's argument that in nature everything is united. Lines 11, 12 (second octave) suggest a rejection of the argument is unforgivable. Final lines ask what is the value of unity if the lover will not unite with the speaker.

Structure: The rhyme scheme *ababcdcd* works with the rhythm to create a light harmonious movement, reflecting the optimistic **theme** of romantic love.

SUMMARY

- The speaker addresses a potential lover about the nature of love in an attempt to persuade the lover to kiss him.
- He suggests that in nature everything comes in pairs.
- He emphasises these dualities, insisting that this is the natural order of things.
- He goes further and argues that a rejection of this duality is unforgiveable.
- Because nothing in nature is single it is appropriate that he and the woman should be together, he suggests. If they are not, what is the value of all these pairings in nature, he asks?

KEY ASPECTS OF THE POEM

A   The main theme of the poem is **the nature of romantic love**. Another theme is **seduction**.

B   The poem is a lyric poem from the Romantic period, and also an **argument** in the **first person**.

C   Pathetic fallacy is also used to describe aspects of nature.

D   In the poem Love and Nature, **abstract nouns**, are personified.

E   The poem is written in two octaves with a regular rhyme scheme and cadence.

KEY SETTING: A BACKDROP **A02**

Shelley does not tell us where or when the speaker addresses the would-be lover. Instead, the poet creates scenes in which different features of Nature are depicted as communing with one another, so for example, 'fountains mingle with the river/ And the rivers with the Ocean' (1, 2) or 'mountains kiss high Heaven' (9) – a metonym for the sky. The effect of these scenes is to form a backdrop that represents an ideal world, a world in which love is the guiding principle and where everything is in harmony. Within this harmony, however, there is constant change, so that a feature blends into another, transforming itself.

KEY QUOTATION: UNITY **A02**

Shelley uses the last two lines to highlight the main point of the poem as a rhetorical question to support his argument: 'what are all these kissings worth/If though kiss not me?' (15, 16). In other words, none of Nature's pairings are worth anything unless the speaker can unite with the object of his affections.

TOP TIP **A02**

Apart from the key quotation, there is another rhetorical question at the end of verse one. It is different in tone from the key quotation. Try to explain why.

EXAM FOCUS: WRITING ABOUT EFFECTS (A02)

Read what one student has written about how the poet creates effects through imagery.

> A good opening point about the type of imagery

Most of the imagery Shelley creates in the poem comes from Nature's four elements: earth, fire, water and air. He presents them as features of the natural world that are paired with each other, so that 'waves clasp one another' or 'sunlight clasps the earth'. In addition verbs such as 'clasp' and 'kiss' personify the features as though they were lovers, and the love between them is 'a law divine', meaning it is sacred. The effect of this duality throughout the poem is that the reader feels that Shelley's argument that two people should come together to love one another is natural, and therefore to reject it is ...

> A sound example of a literary technique that is also embedded in the sentence

> A useful connective to highlight an extra point

> A good reference to the effects Shelley creates

Now you try it:

Complete the last sentence, showing how the lovers are like the features of Nature in the poem.

KEY TECHNIQUE: A LIGHT MOVEMENT (A02)

The poem is written in two octaves. The simple rhyme scheme *ababcdcd* works together with the easy rhythm to produce a light movement. The rhymes, for example 'single/mingle' (5/7) or 'sea/me' (14/16) have a light, rhythmic sound. This is part of the lightness of the voice, and reinforces the optimistic theme of romantic love and the benign movement of the natural world such as water and wind. Frequent enjambment carries an idea from one line to another, as in 'No sister-flower would be forgiven/ If it disdain'd its brother' (11, 12), reinforcing the flowing movement. The dash which occurs towards the end of each stanza acts as a pause and emphasises the line that follows.

> **TOP TIP** (A02)
>
> Repetition is a common technique. Reread the poem and find as many repeated words as you can. What do you think is the overall effect of these on the reader?

> **CHECKPOINT 1** (A02)
>
> What do you think 'Love's Philosophy' is?

Porphyria's Lover

Key technique – pathetic fallacy: The wind takes on human qualities, creating a brooding, sinister effect.

Key technique: Suggests the movement of a ghostly form, foreshadowing Porphyria's death.

Language: The poet contrasts the warmth of the cottage with extreme weather, lulling the reader into a false sense of security.

Key technique – repetition: Helps to build the rhythmical power of the poem, driving the narrative along towards the climax and murder.

Key language: Image suggests Porphyria's physical beauty and the speaker's desire to possess her.

Key language: Suggests speaker is passive, self-pitying. Sees himself as powerless?

Key technique: Image of malevolent weather hints at the violence to come

Form and viewpoint – dramatic monologue: A single voice/narrator creates a strong sense of character.

Structure: The regular rhyme helps to move the narrative along.

Key technique: A key image is often repeated, representing beauty, desire and death.

Language: Suggests Porphyria has another life beyond the cottage.

Language: Suggests Porphyria is affluent, which contrasts with the speaker's life.

The rain set early in to-night,
    The sullen wind was soon awake,
It tore the elm-tops down for spite,
    And did its worst to vex the lake:
5   I listened with heart fit to break.
When glided in Porphyria; straight
    She shut the cold out and the storm,
And kneeled and made the cheerless grate
    Blaze up, and all the cottage warm;
10   Which done, she rose, and from her form
Withdrew the dripping cloak and shawl,
    And laid her soiled gloves by, untied
Her hat and let the damp hair fall,
    And, last, she sat down by my side
15   And called me. When no voice replied,
She put my arm about her waist,
    And made her smooth white shoulder bare,
And all her yellow hair displaced,
    And, stooping, made my cheek lie there,
20   And spread, o'er all, her yellow hair,
Murmuring how she loved me – she
    Too weak, for all her heart's endeavour,
To set its struggling passion free
    From pride, and vainer ties dissever,
25   And give herself to me for ever.
But passion sometimes would prevail,
    Nor could tonight's gay feast restrain
A sudden thought of one so pale
    For love of her, and all in vain:
30   So, she was come through wind and rain.
Be sure I looked up at her eyes

Key language: Suggests the speaker has convinced himself that Porphyria's visit reveals not only love, but devotion, also suggesting he is unbalanced.

Key technique: Image suggests the hangman's noose. Is the speaker punishing Porphyria for her other life?

Key theme: Speaker's blunt recounting emphasises theme of **mental instability**.

Structure: Iambic tetrameter and simple rhyme reinforce the shock of the murder.

Key language: Positions are reversed (see line 19). Porphyria's head rests on the speaker's shoulder, suggesting that he is now in control.

Key technique – ambiguity: The speaker's motives for the crime are uncertain. Is God's approval needed?

Happy and proud; at last I knew

Porphyria worshipped me: surprise

  Made my heart swell, and still it grew

35   While I debated what to do.

That moment she was mine, mine, fair,

  Perfectly pure and good: I found

A thing to do, and all her hair

  In one long **yellow string** I wound

40   Three times her little throat around,

And strangled her. No pain felt she;

  I am quite sure she felt no pain.

As a shut bud that holds a bee,

  I warily oped her lids: **again**

45   Laughed the blue eyes without a **stain**.

And I untightened next the tress

  About her neck; her cheek once more

Blushed bright beneath my burning kiss:

  I propped her head up as before,

50   Only, this time my shoulder bore

Her head, which droops upon it still:

  The smiling rosy little head,

So glad it has its utmost will,

  That all it scorned at once is fled,

55   And I, its love, am gained instead!

Porphyria's love: she guessed not how

  Her darling one wish would be heard.

And thus we sit together now,

  And all night long we have not stirred,

60   And yet God has not said a word!

Robert Browning (1812–1889)

Viewpoint: Unreliable, since Porphyria has no voice.

Voice: Although the speaker narrates events there is no dialogue with Porphyria. Events are recounted through his thoughts, suggesting intensity and obsession.

Key technique: A powerful **simile** of imprisonment and death.

Context: A macabre image of the speaker drawn to the corpse, reminiscent of **Gothic horror**.

Theme: Porphyria's death and passivity depict **female subjection**.

SUMMARY

- The speaker looks back at the events that night, telling how Porphyria, the woman he loves, arrives during a storm.
- He describes how she makes a fire, takes off her wet outer garments and sits next to him, placing his arm around her waist.
- We are told that her wet hair falls across her bare shoulder where she places the speaker's cheek, and she whispers her love for him.
- Despite her passion, she will not give in to him; she has other ties.
- The speaker nonetheless believes that Porphyria adores him.
- He describes how he winds her hair three times around her throat and strangles her. He claims she feels no pain.
- He describes his feelings of happiness at possessing her.
- Finally, he props her lifeless head on his shoulder and sits quietly, surprised that God has not yet spoken.

KEY ASPECTS OF THE POEM

A The speaker recounts the narrative directly to the reader. The poem is a dramatic monologue.

B The calm, colloquial speech in which the speaker tells the horrific events suggests he is **out of touch with reality**. The themes are **perverse love** and **mental instability**.

C The speaker's actions and attitudes also reveal the **theme** of **women's subjection**.

D We do not know the speaker's **motives** for the crime, which make them ambiguous.

E The disturbing and transgressive nature of the poem also places it in the **Gothic** genre (see **Part Three: Contexts**).

F The poem has a regular rhyme scheme and is written in iambic tetrameter.

KEY SETTING: INSIDE AND OUT (A02)

There are two settings in the poem. The first is a storm, a series of violent images in which Browning uses **pathetic fallacy**. The 'sullen wind' (2) rips the 'elm-tops' (3) out of 'spite' (3) and does 'its worst to vex the lake' (4). These malevolent descriptions, coupled with the motionless speaker inside the cottage who listens 'with heart fit to break' (5), create an unsettling effect. Does it hint at something distressing to come? If so, we cannot guess how disturbing this will in fact be.

The second setting is the interior of the cottage. It contrasts with the disorder outside and appears calm and undisturbed, if dismal. When Porphyria enters she not only has the power to shut out the external chaos, but also to bring warmth by making 'the cheerless grate/Blaze up' (8, 9). Browning creates a false impression that the cottage is a place of safety.

KEY CONTEXT (A03)

Robert Browning (1812–89) was a famous Victorian poet and playwright, married to the poet Elizabeth Barrett Browning. He is known for his dramatic monologues, many of which make observations about the condition of Victorian society. 'Porphyria's Lover' may have been influenced by a famous murder, in which the murdered woman had hair much like Porphyria's 'yellow hair' (18).

CHECKPOINT 2 (A01)

How would you interpret the final line of the poem?

KEY CONTEXT **A03**

An article published in 'Extracts from Gosschen's Diary', *Blackwood's Magazine* (1818) about the murder of a woman who had 'radiant golden hair' similar to Porphyria's may well have influenced Browning's choice of subject.

TOP TIP **A02**

Notice how the dramatic monologue allows Browning to highlight ambiguity in this poem, because we only hear the events through the speaker, not Porphyria. The speaker is out of touch with reality, so he is unreliable and we cannot be sure that what he says is to be trusted.

TOP TIP **A01**

Porphyria is a visitor to the cottage. The 'vainer ties' (24) she has refer to her life beyond the cottage. Find evidence in the poem that gives clues as to what this life might be like.

TOP TIP: WRITING ABOUT THE SPEAKER AND PORPHYRIA **A01**

It's important that you can write about the dynamic between Porphyria and the speaker. Although in control of the story through the dramatic monologue, the speaker is a passive character for the first part of the poem. He is immobile, while Porphyria is active. She sits beside him, guides his actions and tends to him, to 'one so pale/For love of her' (28, 29), suggesting that he is lovesick, perhaps ill. His love, he adds, is hopeless. Does she not truly love him? Is she unable to give him what he wants? A few lines further on the speaker becomes convinced that Porphyria worships him. This drives him to enact his plan and the moment before she dies, she becomes all his: 'mine, mine' (36). Now he possesses his ideal woman, 'Perfectly pure and good' (37).

AIMING HIGH: MOTIVES

You will gain higher marks if you can explore the speaker's motives beyond his need to possess Porphyria. As a corpse, Porphyria is as passive as it is possible to be. She belongs to the speaker 'for ever' (25). In other words the speaker is able to control her entirely. Porphyria will never change, never be drawn to those unspecified 'vainer ties' (24) that seem to threaten his relationship with her. He has also convinced himself that this is what she wanted: 'Her darling one wish' (57). Whether or not Porphyria 'worshipped' (33) the speaker (the word implies god-like devotion), he can maintain the macabre belief that she will do so until the end of time. We could argue that in this respect he has become, in his own mind, a god.

Form/Structure: A love song in the form of a Petrarchan sonnet – the octave presents the problem or situation, the volta is the turning point, the sestet presents the resolution.

Context: An example of Victorian love poetry, from *Sonnets of the Portuguese,* dedicated to the poet's husband Robert Browning.

Sonnet 29 – 'I think of thee!'

Voice: First person, addresses the absent lover urgently, passionately.

Key technique: A metaphor for vine leaves, indicating the rambling nature of the speaker's feelings.

Key technique: A metaphor for the masculine lover, portraying strength.

Themes: Passionate love expressed.

Language: Nature imagery is used to create a sensual image.

Sound – alliteration: The 'd', is a heavy, downward sound, emphasising meaning.

I think of thee! – my thoughts do twine and bud

About thee, as wild vines, about a tree,

Put out broad leaves, and soon there's nought to see

Except the straggling green which hides the wood.

5   Yet, O my palm-tree, be it understood

I will not have my thoughts instead of thee

Who art dearer, better! Rather, instantly

Renew thy presence; as a strong tree should,

Rustle thy boughs and set thy trunk all bare,

10   And let these bands of greenery which insphere thee

Drop heavily down, – burst, shattered, everywhere!

Because, in this deep joy to see and hear thee

And breathe within thy shadow a new air,

I do not think of thee – I am too near thee.

Elizabeth Barrett Browning (1806–1861)

Key technique – simile: Uses nature imagery, showing how thoughts about the lover cling and increase.

Language: Suggests that thoughts overwhelm, so the image of the lover is lost.

Structure: Iambic pentameter makes the voice seem natural, fluent.

Key technique – volta: A turning point in a sonnet; the speaker calls on the lover to appear.

Sound – assonance: The 'e' draws attention to this line to contrast with the following line.

Key technique – caesura: A pause works with alliteration to add emphasis.

Key technique – enjambment: The idea continued into the next line helps to make the voice seem natural.

Key technique: The ending contradicts the beginning (antithesis) to show the speaker and lover united (resolution).

Context: The poet's choice of 'vine' is appropriate; vine was called 'lovestone' during the 19th century because it clung to stone walls.

KEY CONTEXT **A03**

Elizabeth Barrett Browning (1806–61) is an important Victorian poet who suffered ill-health, but nonetheless actively opposed slavery and child labour, and was concerned about the position of women. The poem comes from *Sonnets from the Portuguese*. The volume is considered to have autobiographical links, because they are addressed to her husband, the poet Robert Browning, who wrote 'Porphyria's Lover'.

SUMMARY

- The speaker is preoccupied by thoughts of the one she loves.
- She describes how these thoughts seem to cling to him and multiply so that the image of him in her mind's eye is almost blotted out.
- She would far rather he was with her. Then she would not have this profusion of thoughts.
- She calls him to come to her.
- If he were near, her thoughts would be scattered.
- His presence would mean she would have no need to think of him.

KEY ASPECTS OF THE POEM

- **A** The poem is a **Petrarchan sonnet** written in two **quatrains** (or an **octave**) and a **sestet** told in the **first person** and addressed to the loved one.
- **B** It is also a **lyric** poem.
- **C** Its main themes are **passionate love** and **separation**.
- **D** It uses striking **images** from **nature**.
- **E** The **voice** is passionate and seems **autobiographical**.

KEY SETTING: A VICTORIAN IMAGINATION

Elizabeth Barrett Browning chooses no concrete setting for her sonnet, and we can only imagine the speaker as a woman from the Victorian period writing to her lover. The events or the poet's ideas are acted out in the speaker's mind, which is teeming with imagery that depicts the natural world of trees and vines. This imagery creates a backdrop for the reader.

KEY LANGUAGE: VINE AND TREE **A02**

In the first two lines, the poet chooses a **simile** from the natural world to convey the intensity of the speaker's love, whose thoughts are like 'wild vines' (2) – an appropriate image to convey the clinging nature of these thoughts. Not only do they cling to the 'tree' (2), the **metaphor** that represents the masculine lover and conveys robustness and solidity, but they also grow abundantly. They create foliage that engulfs the tree. The speaker asks the loved one to appear. So the tree must 'Rustle' (9) its branches to shake off 'these bands of greenery' (10) – a metaphor for ridding the speaker of her profuse thoughts. Once the tree has lost the foliage the speaker will be able to breathe fresh air again. In other words, her thoughts will no longer be needed because the lover will be present.

⭐ AIMING HIGH: EXPLORING LOVE

Notice how Elizabeth Barrett Browing has chosen the Petrarchan sonnet form to explore the nature of love when lovers are separated. You can follow the shifts in meaning through the movement of the poem. Broadly, it lays out the concern or argument in the first quatrain and explores and develops it in the second. Finally in the sestet there is a change in the argument, idea or tone, and a resolution or final comment; this shift is called a volta. To gain

more marks you could explore the effects produced by the volta. What is the shift like? Does it take the poem to an appropriate resolution? How does it relate to the poem as a whole? You could also consider whether or not the sonnet form the poet has chosen is a satisfactory one to convey the feelings she wants to express.

KEY VOICE: PASSION AND URGENCY **A02**

The poet creates a passionate voice from the very beginning. The first words, 'I think of thee!' (1) are punctuated with an exclamation mark to convey sincerity, and to emphasise the verb 'think' (1), because it is the speaker's thoughts of her lover that consume her. It is also an intimate voice, suggested by the vines that cling to the tree. As the speaker describes her need for her lover's presence the voice becomes more urgent. The speaker's feelings must be 'understood' (5) and her 'thoughts' (6) are no substitute for his absence. 'Renew thy presence' (8) she demands, and the poem ends with a passionate declaration of her sense of 'deep joy' (12) when he is near.

KEY QUOTATION: THE FINAL LINE **A02**

Read on its own, the final line 'I do not think of thee – I am too near thee' (14) might seem contrary. However, there is no real contradiction, for in the final line the poet no longer needs to be overwhelmed by thoughts of her absent lover once he is present. The first six words in the final line also contrast with the opening words, 'I think of thee!' (1), where she is overwhelmed with thoughts of him in his absence. Inevitably we are drawn back to these opening words, and the poet may even have intended that we return to it to create a particular effect. Put together they form an antithesis: 'I think of thee!' 'I do not think of thee …' (1, 14).

> **TOP TIP** **A01**
>
> The nature of poetry is such that its meanings are rarely obvious and a great deal is open to interpretation. When you are writing about poetry it is always best to use verbs such as 'imply', 'suggest', 'infer' or 'assume'.

> **TOP TIP** **A02**
>
> Remember that if a metaphor continues through the lines of the poem it becomes an extended metaphor. Reread the poem and decide whether the metaphor of the vine becomes an extended metaphor – and if so, how.

Key language: Choice of words suggests inactivity, lifelessness; mirrors the relationship.

Theme: The speaker recalls a **memory**, looks back to an event.

Form: Four quatrains and a simple, regular rhyme scheme – reflects the idea of neutrality.

Language: Nature imagery; the sun is bleached of life.

Neutral Tones

We **stood** by a pond that winter day,

And the sun was white, as though chidden[1] of God,

And a few leaves **lay** on the **starving sod**;

    – They had fallen from an **ash**, and were grey.

Key technique: Nature imagery; the earth is personified as dying.

Language: Double meaning: 'ash' is a tree and the remnants of a fire, suggesting the **theme** as the death of the relationship.

Form: The line set apart (in all quatrains) as though the stanza is imperfect, like the relationship.

Viewpoint: First person speaker who addresses an unnamed person present in the poem.

5   Your eyes on me were as eyes that rove

    Over tedious riddles of years ago;

    And some words played between us to and fro

      On which lost the more by our love.

Key technique – enjambment: Line runs on into next for emphasis.

Language: Suggests resentment/unresolved complaints that undermined relationship.

Structure: The rhythm of the line falters, emphasising a poor relationship.

Key technique – ambiguity: Were the words spoken trivial, tiresome ... what?

    The smile on your mouth was the deadest thing

10   Alive enough to have strength to die;

    And a grin of bitterness swept thereby

      Like an ominous bird a-wing…

Key technique – ambiguity: Strong feelings expressed; is this at odds with 'neutral' feelings?

Key technique – simile: Compares 'grin' to a sinister bird, with connotations of malice.

Sound: The sibilant creates a hissing sound, suggesting slyness.

Viewpoint: The speaker shifts from past memory to present time.

    Since then, **k**een le**ss**ons that love de**c**eives,

    And wrings with wrong, have shaped to me

15   Your face, and the God-curst sun, and a tree,

      And a pond edged with greyish leaves.

Sound: The harsh 'k' emphasises 'keen', meaning 'sharp' as well as 'earnest', which reflects the nature of the relationship.

Structure: A conclusive ending, but no resolution, suggesting the relationship remains lifeless as in stanza one.

Thomas Hardy (1840–1928)

Key technique – caesura: The pause emphasises the line as it runs into 'Your face', highlighting feelings of bitterness.

Glossary

[1] chidden = scorned

SUMMARY

- The poem opens as the speaker recalls a particular memory: he and another person (we may assume a lover) are near a pond and a tree in winter.

- He remembers that the other person looks at him as though remembering unresolved grievances. They exchange a few words that are either insignificant, or words that have been said many times before.

- He recalls that the other person's smile was cold and bitter.

- The speaker moves forward in time to consider what love means and how it creates untrustworthy feelings.

- These feelings are associated with the other person's face and the memory of that austere day.

KEY ASPECTS OF THE POEM

A   The main theme is the **death of love**. Other related themes are **regret**, **loss** and **memory**.

B   The poem is written in four quatrains. It has a simple rhyme scheme. It is told in the **first person** and addressed to the other person.

C   The **rhythm** of the poem seems **regular at first**, **but is broken**, most frequently in the last line of each verse.

D   The images in the poem are bleak.

KEY SETTING: A BLEAK VIEW   (A02)

CHECKPOINT 3   (A02)

Do you think the title 'Neutral Tones' suits the poem?

Hardy creates a bleak setting, formed as a memory in the mind of the speaker, whose surroundings are dead or famished, from the 'grey' (4) leaves to the 'starving sod' (3). This final image is a **personification**, a technique that makes the desolate relationship more vivid in the reader's mind. The tree has **connotations** of death and the remnants of fire, suggesting that any passion has gone. The sun seems bleached 'white' (2) as though it has been 'chidden of God' (2) and lost its force. With these images of death and dying comes stillness. There is no indication that the water in the pond is moving, and the leaves have already fallen. Again, the reader is reminded that the relationship has ceased.

EXAM FOCUS: WRITING ABOUT EFFECTS   (A02)

Read what one student has written about the form and rhythm of the poem and how this creates effects.

> Hardy uses an uncomplicated form for the poem, four quatrains with a simple regular rhyme scheme, *abba*. The effect of this repetition stresses the low-key tone, which is mirrored in the title, 'Neutral Tones'. However, the last line of each verse is set apart from the others. The effect of this technique reminds the reader of the separation between the speaker and the other person. Also, when we read the last line we pause, and it is almost like a sigh, as though the speaker is expressing his sadness or resentment at the relationship. Another feature is that the regular rhythm is broken in lines such as 'And some words played between us to and fro', so that it jars slightly.

Thorough use of literary techniques used by Hardy to create effects

An appropriate way of describing the reader's emotional response to the line

A quotation successfully embedded in the sentence

Now you try it:

Add a sentence to say what the effect is of the broken rhythm on our understanding of the relationship between the speaker and the other person.

KEY THEME: THE DEATH OF LOVE   (A02)

CHECKPOINT 4   (A01)

What do you think the line 'On which lost the more by our love' (8) could mean?

As well as presenting the main theme through the desolate images of the landscape, Hardy also presents it through the speaker's observations of the other person in the poem. The other person's 'smile' is the 'deadest thing' (9), while the **simile** 'grin of bitterness' 'like an ominous bird' (11, 12) makes the other person seem malevolent. One of the starkest images is in the last verse. When we read that 'love deceives/And wrings with wrong, have shaped to me' (13, 14) we must run on to the next line carrying the image with us, to read 'Your face' (15). It has a disturbing effect, and it sits so close to the image of 'the God-curst sun' (15) that it is inevitably linked.

Sound – alliteration: Heavy 'p' sound accentuates heavy soil and manual work.

Letters from Yorkshire

Viewpoint: Speaker addresses the reader about a friend.

Theme – communication: Links to poem's title.

Theme: Suggests **friendship** as theme rather than romantic love.

Viewpoint: Speaker shifts to addressing friend, increases sense of intimacy between them.

Key technique – ambiguity: 'heartful' is a constructed word. News headlines troubling? Speaker weary of writing about news? Also suggests that the speaker's 'heart'/emotions are preoccupied with her friend.

Sound: **End** and **internal rhymes** create **cadence**, and help **voice** sound like natural speech.

Key technique – enjambment: Runs idea on to next stanza, hinting that speaker would like a rural life?

Key technique – key image: Communication between friends and communicating with nature.

Language: Suggests a deep emotional bond.

In February, digging his garden, **p**lanting **p**otatoes,

he saw the first lapwings return and came

indoors to write to me, his knuckles singing

as they reddened in the warmth.

5   It's not romance, simply how things are.

You out there, in the cold, **see**ing the **seas**ons

turning, me with my heartful of headlines

feeding words onto a blank screen.

Is your life more real because you dig and **sow**?

10   You wouldn't say **so**, breaking ice on a waterbutt,

clearing a path through **snow**. Still, it's you

who sends me word of that other world

pouring air and light into an envelope. So that

at night, watching the same news in different houses,

15   our souls tap out messages across the icy miles.

Maura Dooley (1957–)

Sound: 'ing' repeated in stanza one helps to conjure the ring of the spade.

Language: Moving from outdoors to indoors (cold to warmth) to write to the speaker suggests the relationship is warming him too.

Sound: Sibilance ('s') repeated with assonance ('ee') highlights the desire for the natural world.

Theme: Contrast between **urban life/ rural life; nature**.

Voice: Colloquial speech, as though speaker is chatting to a friend.

Context: Suggests the shift in society from working outside on the land to inside working at a computer screen and from letter writing to emails.

Key technique – caesura: Pause emphasises a key image.

Language: Reminds us of semaphore, reinforcing the idea of the theme of 'communication'.

Structure: Strong ending in which the friends seem closer despite the distance.

KEY CONTEXT (A03)

Maura Dooley (b. 1957) is of Irish descent. She was born in Cornwall and lived in Bristol as a child. She has had several volumes of poetry published. Two volumes, *Kissing A Bone* (1996) and *Life Underwater* (2008) were shortlisted for the T. S. Eliot Prize. She attended the University of York and worked in Yorkshire.

SUMMARY

- We assume the speaker is a woman. She is recalling the circumstances in which her friend or lover writes to her.
- She remembers that it is February and that his life is in rural Yorkshire. He works in the open air and notes the features of the season.
- She imagines the two of them in their contrasting situations. He is a gardener. She is typing on her keyboard, thinking about the news, and she asks whose life is more real.
- She claims he would not consider his life to be more real than hers. Nonetheless, in his letters he sends her a sense of what it is to be outdoors in the countryside.
- They both, in their separate houses, are watching the same news and are joined together through their words.

KEY ASPECTS OF THE POEM

A   The main themes are **communication** and **love** or **close friendship**. Another theme is **nature,** and **urban/rural life**.
B   The poem is written in five tercets. There is a shift in who is being addressed.
C   It is a free verse poem, with some internal rhymes.
D   It has many run-on lines.
E   The images are mainly **rural**.

KEY SETTING: OUTDOORS AND INDOORS   (A02)

The poem has two contrasting settings. It opens with a simple image of Yorkshire in February as the speaker describes the other person, 'digging his garden' (1). When he steps indoors to write a letter to her, 'his knuckles singing/as they reddened in the warmth' (3, 4) the poet creates a tactile reminder of the wintry season. In verse three we move to the speaker's circumstances, which are at odds with the rural image. It is an indoor setting in which the speaker is sedentary, 'feeding words onto a blank screen' (8), which suggests that her working life is unrewarding. She knows the other person's life is full of activity and close

to nature – he details how 'he saw the first lapwings return' (2). So 'Is [his] life more real' (9)? She asks this rhetorical question, and doubts that he would say it was, but we are left with the impression that the speaker feels a longing for 'that other world' (12).

KEY QUOTATION: THE RURAL WORLD IN AN ENVELOPE (A02)

There is an important quotation in the fourth verse, 'Still, it's you/who sends me word of that other world' (11, 12) which runs on into the final verse, to read 'pouring air and light into an envelope' (13). Through the imagery of the abundant fresh air and the sunlight the poet creates the effect that the rural world is contained in the envelope through the letter-writer's words. So a bridge is made between the other person's world and the speaker's. In addition the poet highlights this bridge through **enjambment** between the two verses, reinforcing the connection.

KEY TECHNIQUE: THE SENSES (A02)

Dooley has chosen a conversational tone for the poem, but while the language seems natural she uses certain techniques to create striking effects. As in much free verse there are hidden rhymes in the poem. The effect of 'digging', 'planting' (1) and 'singing' (3) is to hear the ring of the spade against a stone, a common experience for a gardener. The same effect occurs in verse four when the gardener is 'breaking ice on a waterbutt' (10). The **alliterative** 'p' in 'planting potatoes' (1) reminds us of heavy boots on soil, and the sheer pleasure of saying 'seeing the seasons' (6) (in which **assonance** as well as the **sibilant** is used) stresses the pleasure the gardener must feel in his work.

KEY THEME: LONG-DISTANCE LINKS (A01)

The poet focuses on the theme of communication in its widest sense. The title 'Letters from Yorkshire' indicates one form of simple communication through the postal service. Typing on a computer and hearing the news are two more. Communing with the natural world, as the letter writer does when he sees 'the first lapwings return' (2) is yet another form. However, the most important communication is the connection between the two people at an emotional level. The letter-writer's need to record and send his observations is an example of the love or closeness of the relationship, despite the geographical distance between them. And the use of the word 'souls' in the speaker's final comment 'our souls tap out messages across the icy miles' (15) suggests that the emotional bond between the two is deep.

REVISION FOCUS: CONTRASTS

Reread 'Letters from Yorkshire'. Note as many contrasts as you can, and consider the circumstances of the different lives. Identify important quotations as evidence to support what you say. Draw up a two-column table headed 'Contrasts' and 'Evidence', and use it to record your observations.

TOP TIP (A01)

Notice the image 'my heartful of headlines' (7). 'Heartful' is a constructed word that could mean 'hearfelt', implying that the news headlines are troubling, or that the speaker is weary of the depressing nature of the headlines. Also, we often speak of the 'heart or the head' as though they were opposites. What might the speaker be saying?

TOP TIP (A01)

In verse two the word 'romance' (5) is used. This can refer to romantic love or it can mean sentiment, or it can refer to a feeling of mystery. Sometimes words can have subtle shifts in meaning, usually depending on the context in which they are written. These different meanings can cast a new light on the text.

Key technique:
Foreshadowing used to hint at marriage problems and the farmer's disappointment in his wife.

Theme: The wife rejects her marriage and husband, suggesting **unrequited love**.

Key technique – simile: 'shut' reinforces the **theme** of rejection and unrequited love, 'winter' the theme of coldness in the relationship.

Context: Archaic language sets the poem in the nineteenth century.

Form: The layout of the line reflects the long chase across the landscape.

Language: The wife is portrayed as a hunted animal, suggesting her inferior position.

Structure: Line shifts to present tense and the narrative becomes more immediate.

Language: The imagery suggests the wife has an affinity with animals.

The Farmer's Bride

Three Summers since I chose a maid,

Too young maybe – but more's to do

At harvest-time than bide[1] and woo.

When us was wed she turned afraid

5   Of love and me and all things human;

Like the shut of a winter's day

Her smile went out, and 'twasn't a woman –

More like a little frightened fay.[2]

One night, in the Fall, she runned away.

10 'Out 'mong the sheep, her be,' they said,

Should properly have been abed;

But sure enough she wasn't there

Lying awake with her wide brown stare.

So over seven-acre field and up-along across the down

15 We chased her, flying like a hare

Before our lanterns. To Church-Town

All in a shiver and a scare

We caught her , fetched her home at last

And turned the key upon her, fast.

20 She does the work about the house

As well as most, but like a mouse:

Happy enough to chat and play

With birds and rabbits and such as they,

So long as men-folk keep away.

Viewpoint: First person **narrator** (farmer) recalls event of three years ago.

Language: In suggesting his wife is at odds with the human world, the speaker depicts her as strange, an outsider.

Structure: A **rhyming couplet** closes the first four **stanzas**, as the **narrative** unfolds, rather like the close of chapters in a novel.

Language: Conjures an image of the wife as a wide-eyed fearful creature – a doe or fawn.

Context: The historical detail and naming of the town helps to build a credible narrative.

Context: The farmer's actions would have been acceptable at the time the poem is set.

Form: A **lament** in six rhyming verses. The simple song-like rhymes reflect the traditional, rural setting.

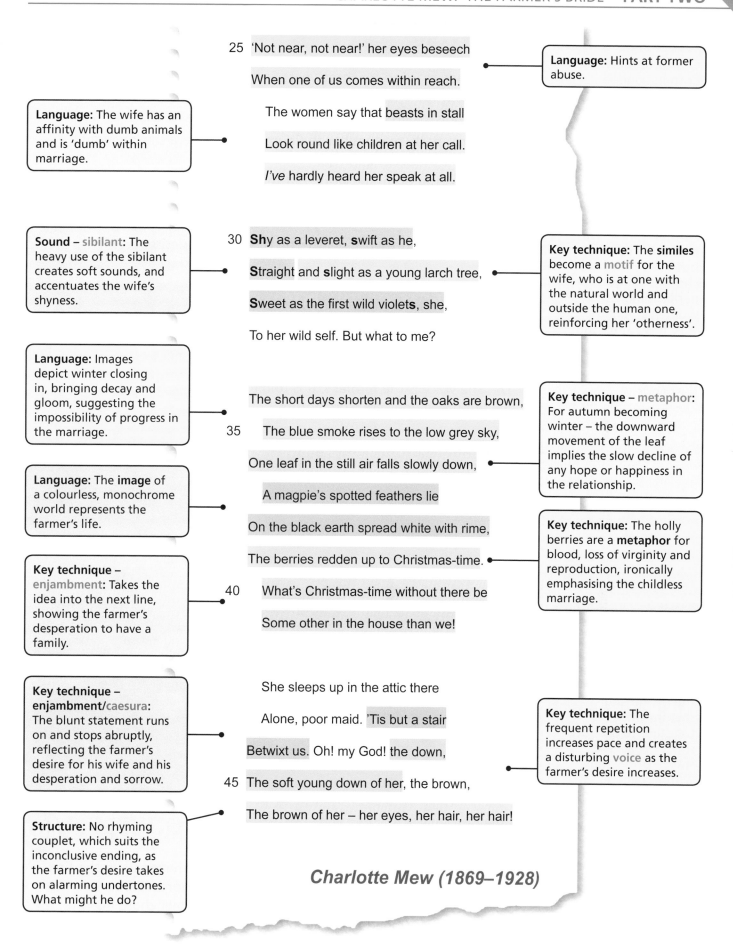

Language: The wife has an affinity with dumb animals and is 'dumb' within marriage.

Sound – sibilant: The heavy use of the sibilant creates soft sounds, and accentuates the wife's shyness.

Language: Images depict winter closing in, bringing decay and gloom, suggesting the impossibility of progress in the marriage.

Language: The **image** of a colourless, monochrome world represents the farmer's life.

Key technique – enjambment: Takes the idea into the next line, showing the farmer's desperation to have a family.

Key technique – enjambment/caesura: The blunt statement runs on and stops abruptly, reflecting the farmer's desire for his wife and his desperation and sorrow.

Structure: No rhyming couplet, which suits the inconclusive ending, as the farmer's desire takes on alarming undertones. What might he do?

Language: Hints at former abuse.

Key technique: The **similes** become a motif for the wife, who is at one with the natural world and outside the human one, reinforcing her 'otherness'.

Key technique – metaphor: For autumn becoming winter – the downward movement of the leaf implies the slow decline of any hope or happiness in the relationship.

Key technique: The holly berries are a **metaphor** for blood, loss of virginity and reproduction, ironically emphasising the childless marriage.

Key technique: The frequent repetition increases pace and creates a disturbing **voice** as the farmer's desire increases.

25 'Not near, not near!' her eyes beseech

When one of us comes within reach.

The women say that beasts in stall

Look round like children at her call.

I've hardly heard her speak at all.

30 **Sh**y as a leveret, **s**wift as he,

Straight and **s**light as a young larch tree,

Sweet as the first wild violet**s**, she,

To her wild self. But what to me?

The short days shorten and the oaks are brown,

35   The blue smoke rises to the low grey sky,

One leaf in the still air falls slowly down,

   A magpie's spotted feathers lie

On the black earth spread white with rime,

The berries redden up to Christmas-time.

40   What's Christmas-time without there be

Some other in the house than we!

She sleeps up in the attic there

   Alone, poor maid. 'Tis but a stair

Betwixt us. Oh! my God! the down,

45 The soft young down of her, the brown,

The brown of her – her eyes, her hair, her hair!

Charlotte Mew (1869–1928)

Glossary

1   bide = sit waiting

2   fay = fairy

Charlotte Mew was born in London in 1869. She suffered from depression and committed suicide in 1928. A poet who was largely overlooked in her lifetime, she has gained recognition more recently. 'The Farmer's Bride' was published in 1916, but the setting Mew chooses suggests an earlier time when women still had very few rights and were mainly under the supervision of their fathers or husbands.

SUMMARY

- A farmer, married for three years, is dismayed by his loveless relationship.
- His wife is afraid of him and runs away into the fields.
- A search party pursues her to Church-Town where she is caught, taken home and locked up.
- She does her domestic work, but fearing men, can only respond to the animals around her.
- The farmer is drawn to her youth and beauty and longs for a child.
- Aware of her presence nearby, he is filled with desire.

KEY ASPECTS OF THE POEM

A   The poem is a narrative.
B   It is also a lament written in **six rhyming verses**.
C   The theme is **unrequited love**.
D   The voice is the **farmer's**; it is told in the **first person**, in dialect.
E   All the images are from **nature**.

Notice how the stanzas have a complex and varying rhyme scheme, and the rhyme and rhythm work together to produce shifts in pace. A stanza often ends with a rhyming couplet that brings it to a satisfactory close. One exception is the last stanza. Note how it seems to end in mid-air and has the effect of accentuating both the rhythm and the sinister tone. It also challenges our expectations, so that we are left wondering what will happen next.

KEY SETTING: NATURE AND THE SEASONS   **A02**

The poem has a vivid rural setting. Each season is referred to. In the first verse the setting is harvest time, and the opening words 'Three Summers' (1) signifies the years that have passed since the farmer chose his wife. Spring is not mentioned by name, but Mew suggests it in images such as 'the first wild violets' (32). As autumn progresses the poem becomes bleaker, giving way to winter's 'black earth' (38). The only colour in this monochrome world is red, the berries of Christmas, a **metaphor** for blood and loss of virginity, and also for reproduction, reminding us of the farmer's childless marriage.

KEY CHARACTER: WRITING ABOUT THE YOUNG WIFE **A02**

The young wife has no voice, which emphasises her powerlessness. Her affinity with the dumb animals is expressed in **similes**. She is 'like a little frightened fay' (8), 'shy as a leveret' (30) or 'flying like a hare' (15), images that build to create a **motif** of a creature at odds with the human world. She is afraid of the farmer, and all men: has some former mistreatment or abuse occurred?

EXAM FOCUS: WRITING ABOUT THE VOICE   **A02**

Read what one student has written about the voice Mew creates in the poem.

> A literary technique and example used by Mew to create effects

> A useful connective that qualifies an earlier point

Mew brings the farmer to life through his voice and dialect. For example, using the pronoun 'us' instead of 'we' in the expression 'When us was wed ...' has the effect of creating a rural voice and setting in the reader's mind. The farmer is also given a kind of dignity in images such as, 'Like the shut of a winter's day', to remind us that he feels shut out from his wife's love. However, there is also a disturbing side to his voice when he thinks about her alone and asleep in her attic room, and is aware that there is 'but a stair/Betwixt them'. This suggests ...

> A key quotation successfully embedded in the sentence

Now you try it:

Complete the sentence to explain how the last two lines emphasise the disturbing note in the voice.

TOP TIP: WRITING ABOUT CREATING EFFECTS   **A02**

Mew uses different techniques to create effects and highlight meaning. For example, the final four lines of the third stanza all rhyme, which quickens the pace and accentuates the farmer's desperation. However, there are also commas for pause and emphasis and these, along with **alliteration**, such as the heavy use of the **sibilant** – 'Shy' (30), 'swift' (30), 'Straight' (31) and more – highlight the wife's youthful beauty. Then the final line is split (**caesura**) into two parts by a full stop, skilfully echoing the division between the farmer and his wife as well as the sorrow and desperation he feels.

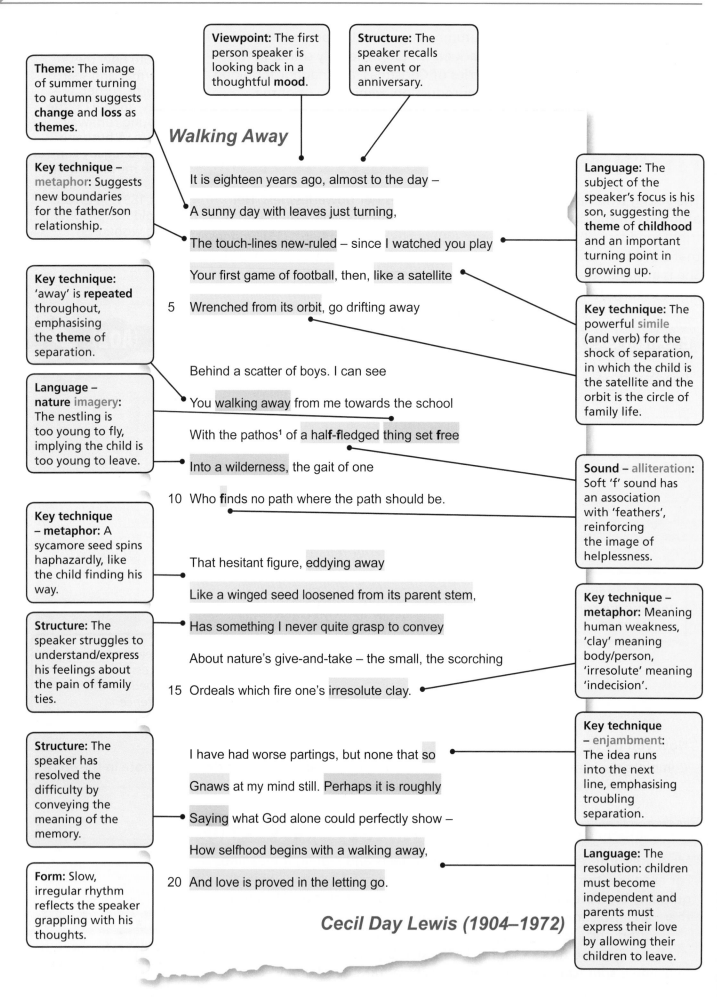

Theme: The image of summer turning to autumn suggests **change** and **loss** as **themes.**

Viewpoint: The first person speaker is looking back in a thoughtful **mood**.

Structure: The speaker recalls an event or anniversary.

Key technique – metaphor: Suggests new boundaries for the father/son relationship.

Key technique: 'away' is **repeated** throughout, emphasising the **theme** of separation.

Language – nature imagery: The nestling is too young to fly, implying the child is too young to leave.

Key technique – metaphor: A sycamore seed spins haphazardly, like the child finding his way.

Structure: The speaker struggles to understand/express his feelings about the pain of family ties.

Structure: The speaker has resolved the difficulty by conveying the meaning of the memory.

Form: Slow, irregular rhythm reflects the speaker grappling with his thoughts.

Walking Away

It is eighteen years ago, almost to the day –

A sunny day with leaves just turning,

The touch-lines new-ruled – since I watched you play

Your first game of football, then, like a satellite

5   Wrenched from its orbit, go drifting away

Behind a scatter of boys. I can see

You walking away from me towards the school

With the pathos[1] of a half-fledged thing set free

Into a wilderness, the gait of one

10   Who finds no path where the path should be.

That hesitant figure, eddying away

Like a winged seed loosened from its parent stem,

Has something I never quite grasp to convey

About nature's give-and-take – the small, the scorching

15   Ordeals which fire one's irresolute clay.

I have had worse partings, but none that so

Gnaws at my mind still. Perhaps it is roughly

Saying what God alone could perfectly show –

How selfhood begins with a walking away,

20   And love is proved in the letting go.

Cecil Day Lewis (1904–1972)

Language: The subject of the speaker's focus is his son, suggesting the **theme** of **childhood** and an important turning point in growing up.

Key technique: The powerful **simile** (and verb) for the shock of separation, in which the child is the satellite and the orbit is the circle of family life.

Sound – alliteration: Soft 'f' sound has an association with 'feathers', reinforcing the image of helplessness.

Key technique – metaphor: Meaning human weakness, 'clay' meaning body/person, 'irresolute' meaning 'indecision'.

Key technique – enjambment: The idea runs into the next line, emphasising troubling separation.

Language: The resolution: children must become independent and parents must express their love by allowing their children to leave.

[1]   pathos = appealing to emotion

SUMMARY

- The poem begins as a father recalls his young son's first game of football.
- He sees his son disappear towards the school after the game.
- The child seems too young to be separated from his father.
- The speaker has difficulty finding the words he needs to describe the experience completely.
- He comments that he has had separations that have been worse, but there is something about this particular memory that haunts him.
- Perhaps, he thinks, the parent expresses his love best by allowing the child to leave and develop his own identity.

KEY ASPECTS OF THE POEM

A   The main themes are **parental love**, **change** and **loss**. Other themes include **separation**, **childhood** and **the natural world**.

B   The poem is written in four quintains.

C   It is written in the **first person** and addressed to the son, making the poem seem **intensely personal**.

D   The **rhyme** is regular, and the **rhythm** is slow and **irregular**.

E   **Enjambment** is frequently used.

KEY SETTING: CHANGE   (A02)

The poet creates a commonplace setting, the moments after a game of children's football, but the speaker recalls it as a potent memory. It is 'A sunny day with leaves just turning' (2), a metaphor for change, as summer slips into autumn and the speaker's son moves into a different stage of his life. His father watches him walk away at the end of the game, as he begins his new school. The situation is new for both of them, just as the 'touch-lines' (3) of the football pitch are 'new-ruled' (3). The 'touch-lines' also imply that the father is outside the son's new world, in the same way that touchlines form a boundary on a pitch. The word 'touch' on its own suggests love; the love that a parent has for a child.

KEY QUOTATION: LETTING GO?   (A01)

The last two lines 'How selfhood begins with a walking away,/And love is proved in the letting go' (19, 20) create more than one effect. The speaker knows that in the normal course of things, his son will become an independent person. A parent, if he loves his child, must let this process happen by 'letting' the child 'go' (20). However, while the speaker knows this, he still feels the loss which 'Gnaws at' his 'mind still' (17). It is a universal feeling shared by all parents.

KEY CONTEXT   (A03)

Cecil Day Lewis (1904–72) was of Irish and English descent and became Poet Laureate (1968–72). Along with W. H. Auden, Stephen Spender and Louis MacNeice he belongs to the group known as the Thirties Poets. His poetry often focuses on the personal, and the poem is dedicated to his son Sean. Day Lewis also wrote detective novels under the pseudonym Nicholas Blake. *C. Day Lewis: The Complete Poems* was published in 1992 by Sinclair Stevenson.

AIMING HIGH: SEPARATION

Notice that throughout the text there is an emphasis on separation embodied in the word 'away': 'drifting away' (5), 'walking away' (7, 19) and 'eddying away' (11), all acted out by the young child as he disappears from his father's sight. The powerful **simile** 'like a satellite/ Wrenched from its orbit' (4, 5) reinforces the theme of separation. The effect of the verb 'wrenched' in particular implies a painful twisting or pulling, so that the separation is a distressing one. There are also other important techniques throughout the poem that underpin the theme, and these work in unison with the language. The rhythm is slow and irregular, highlighting the child's slow 'gait' (9) as he wanders reluctantly towards the school, again suggesting that separation is not easy. The rhyme, which is regular (*abaca*) is also broken by **enjambment**. Notice where this enjambment occurs, and how often. What overall effect does it create?

TOP TIP: WRITING ABOUT THE CHILD (A02)

Remember that the child is seen entirely from the point of view of the speaker, a concerned parent. We assume that he must be young, because he has just played his first game of football and all the **images** of him in the poem suggest vulnerability. Take the striking image of the 'half-fledged thing' (8). It suggests a baby bird that is barely ready to leave the nest. The repeated soft 'f' conjures up in the reader's mind a young bird's feathers or down, adding to the picture of helplessness. The use of 'thing' (8) implies someone who has not yet fully developed into an autonomous person. The child is also 'set free into a wilderness …/Who finds no path where the path should be' (9, 10) – an image of someone who has lost his bearings. Find other images and decide how they add to the overall picture of the child.

CHECKPOINT 6 (A01)

What do you think the image 'the small, the scorching/ Ordeals' (14, 15) refers to?

TOP TIP (A02)

Remember that while there are many **run-on lines** in the poem, there are also several pauses (**caesura**). The longer ones are made using a dash or full stop. Their effect is to create emphasis by halting the reader.

Viewpoint – continuous present: Suggests that the parents are constantly anticipating the speaker's arrival, but are just out of reach.

Key technique: Religious symbol for Paradise, suggesting **theme** of **death** and **afterlife**.

Form: Traditional **quatrains**, of regular full rhyme and half-rhyme, create low-key reflective **mood**.

Eden Rock

They are waiting for me somewhere beyond Eden Rock:

My father, twenty-five, in the same suit

Of Genuine Irish Tweed, his terrier Jack

Still two years old and trembling at his feet.

5 My mother, twenty-three, in a sprigged dress

Drawn at the waist, ribbon in her straw hat,

Has spread the stiff white cloth over the grass.

Her hair, the colour of wheat, takes on the light.

She pours tea from a Thermos, the milk **s**traight

10 From an old H.P. **s**auce bottle, a **s**crew

Of paper for a cork; **s**lowly **s**ets out

The same three plates, the tin cups painted blue.

The sky whitens as if lit by three suns.

My mother shades her eyes and looks my way

15 Over the drifted stream. My father spins

A stone along the water. Leisurely,

They beckon to me from the other bank.

I hear them call, 'See where the stream-path is!

Crossing is not as hard as you might think.'

20 I had not thought that it would be like this.

Charles Causley (1917–2003)

Theme – memory: A distant childhood **memory** of a special day/celebration, suggested by the father's smart clothes.

Language: The image of golden, shining hair suggests a halo, an angelic vision.

Key technique – repetition: 'three' (also in lines 5, 13), a mystical number, reinforces religious imagery.

Language: The sky's brilliance suggests summer heat, and in turn, the speaker's warmth/love for his parents and vice versa.

Key technique – metaphor: 'stream' and 'crossing' suggest crossing the water from life to death.

Viewpoint: Speaker shifts from describing events to addressing the reader directly, creating immediacy.

Language: Imagery of the mother's clothes reinforces a rural setting, perhaps even the idea of the Garden of Eden/Paradise?

Language: Suggests the purity of the cloth (and the memory) and also the memory of a special day.

Sound – alliteration: The sibilant helps create a soft, gentle depiction of the memory.

Key technique – metaphor: The Christian holy trinity (God, Christ, Holy Spirit), holy family (Mary, Joseph, Jesus) and the speaker's family.

Language – imagery: The parents anticipate a reunion (as the speaker does in his imagination), suggesting the **theme** of **parental love**.

Structure: The line set apart further emphasises immediacy and surprise.

KEY CONTEXT (A03)

Charles Causley (1917–2003) wrote poetry for adults and children. Much of his poetry appears simple, but says profound things. He drew on folklore, particularly Cornish, and was interested in ballads, narrative poetry and the mystical. Children often appear in his poetry and innocence is a frequent theme, for example in poems such as 'By St. Thomas Water'. That an innocent child is at the centre of 'Eden Rock' is therefore not surprising.

SUMMARY

- The speaker recalls a family memory.
- He sees his parents in their youth with their dog, having a summer picnic.
- He describes their clothes and the details of the picnic.
- The sun is particularly bright as the speaker's mother looks towards him across a stream and his father spins a stone across the water.
- The speaker's parents call to him to follow the path of the stream so that he can cross over to where they are.
- The speaker does not imagine the experience to be as he thought it would.

KEY ASPECTS OF THE POEM

A   The main themes are **death** and **parental love**. Another theme is **memory**.

B   The poem is written in five quatrains, with the last line set apart.

C   The poem is written in the first person, present tense and in the **continuous present** in the first line.

D   Half-rhyme is used throughout the poem, which has an **irregular rhythm**.

E   Alliteration and assonance are used.

KEY SETTING: PAST AND FUTURE (A01)

The poem's setting is a complex one. The speaker revisits an event from childhood, a family picnic. The 'H.P. sauce bottle' (10) used to hold milk, is stopped by 'a screw/Of paper' (10, 11) and tea is drunk in 'tin cups' (12), dating the memory somewhere between the 1920s and 1940s. However, the speaker's parents 'are waiting for' him 'somewhere beyond Eden Rock' (1), implying that they exist in the poem's present. The descriptions of the events continue to be told in the present tense throughout the poem. Then in the final line the speaker comments on the experience of crossing the stream to meet his parents as though the child and adult have merged. It links closely to the theme of death.

KEY THEME: DEATH AND LOVE (A02)

The poet refers to the Christian religion to explore the main theme of death. The family memory, in which the speaker as a child must cross the 'drifted stream' (15) becomes the speaker imagining himself as an adult crossing from life to death. His parents waiting for him is an expression of their love. It is a brilliant summer's day in which the sky 'whitens' (13), so the reader can assume that the parents are either in Paradise, a place of harmony, or another contented state. The speaker is surprised at the journey, since he 'had not thought that it would be like this' (20), but the 'Crossing', he is told, 'is not as hard' as he 'might think' (19). In the New Testament the idea that adults must become as innocent as children to enter heaven features in several of the gospels (Mark 10:15, Luke 18:17). We can therefore see why the image of crossing the stream as a child was compelling to Causley.

KEY LANGUAGE: RELIGIOUS IMAGERY (A02)

Causley has chosen 'Eden Rock' (1) as a place name. The choice has clear associations with the Garden of Eden in Christianity (and other world religions) and is a **symbol** of Paradise. Possibly another reference to Paradise is the potent, otherwordly image 'The sky whitens as if lit by three suns' (13). The number three is mentioned three times in the poem – 'twenty-three' (5), 'three plates' (12) and 'three suns' (13) – it is a powerful number in many religions. The 'three suns' could therefore be a **metaphor** for the Christian holy trinity (God, Christ and the Holy Spirit). We could also make connections between the speaker's family and the holy family of Mary, Joseph and Jesus, or it may be a metaphor for the moment before death. Those who have undergone a near-death experience have recounted seeing a bright light, along with other phenomena.

CHECKPOINT 7 (A02)

Where does assonance occur for the sound, 'ee', in verses one and two? (Remember to focus on the sound and not the spelling.) How does it affect the way we see the speaker's parents?

REVISION FOCUS: ALLITERATION

Causley draws on alliteration to create effects in the poem. The different sounds created can be soft, hard, smooth, rough and so on. A sound will relate in some way to the meaning of the poem. Reread the poem, and note down as many examples of alliteration as you can. Try to make associations between the quality of the sound and the effect it has in the poem.

Follower

Language: The title applies to both father and son at different times of their lives.

Viewpoint: First person, past tense. The speaker is looking back at his father and his work, suggesting father/son relationship as a **theme**.

My father worked with a horse-plough,

His shoulders globed like a full sail strung

Between the shafts[1] and the furrow.

Key technique: Nautical **simile** suggests the ploughman's shirt billowing in the wind like sails, with the force of the movement and his muscularity; the plough is like the bows of a ship.

Language: The **image** suggests the clicking of a machine.

The horse strained at his clicking tongue.

5   An expert. He would set the wing

Structure – caesura: The sharp full stop emphasises how much the speaker values his father's expertise.

Sound: 'bright' makes association in meaning and sound with light, coupled with the **sibilant** 's' to emphasise the shining metal plate ('sock').

And fit the bright **s**teel-pointed **s**ock.

The sod rolled over without breaking.

Language: Choice of vocabulary presents a perfect action, showing the father's skill.

At the headrig,[2] with a single pluck

Structure – enjambment: The lines run on into new lines and a new **stanza**, mimicking the plough's movement as it turns to come down the field.

Structure: Full rhyme and **half-rhyme** provide regularity (e.g. full rhyme 'sod'/'plod'/half-rhyme 'wake'/'back').

Of reins, the sweating team turned round

10   And back into the land. His eye

Language: Vocabulary choice emphasises perfection and the son's awe of his father.

Narrowed and angled at the ground,

Mapping the furrow exactly.

Structure: Shifts from focus on the father to the son/speaker.

I stumbled in his hob-nailed wake,

Key technique: Double meaning of 'wake', suggesting 'trail' but also 'a vigil for the dead', **foreshadowing** the father's decline.

Fell sometimes on the polished sod;

Language: All the **images** present the father, his horse and plough as one and **bonding with the soil** (theme).

15   Sometimes he rode me on his back

Dipping and rising to his plod.

Language: The present participle 'ing' works with the rhythm of the line and the plough.

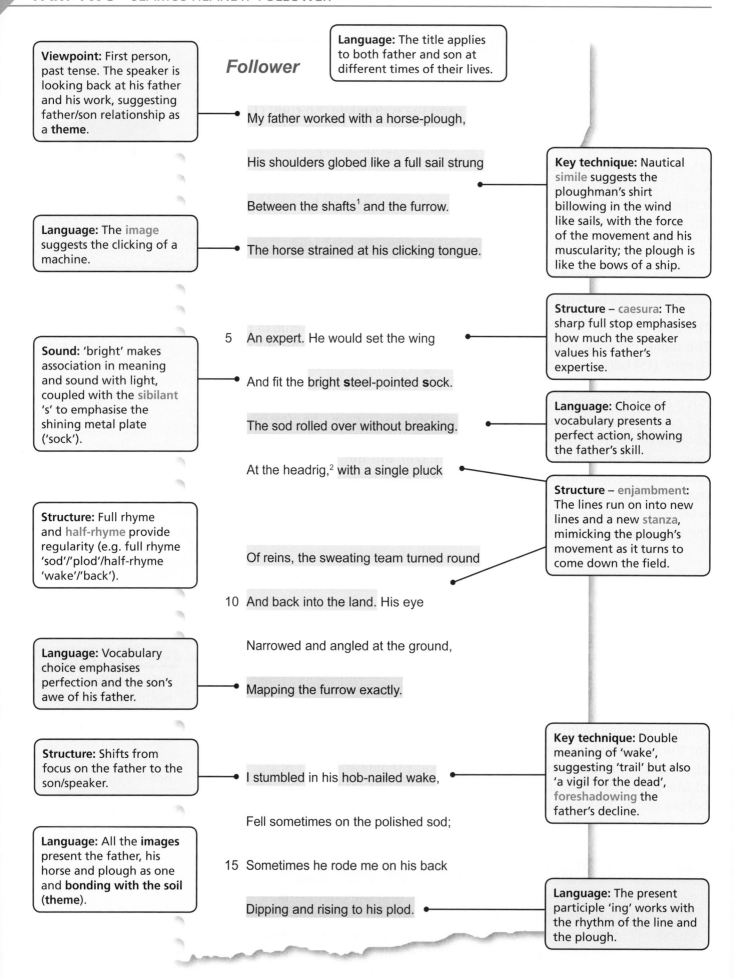

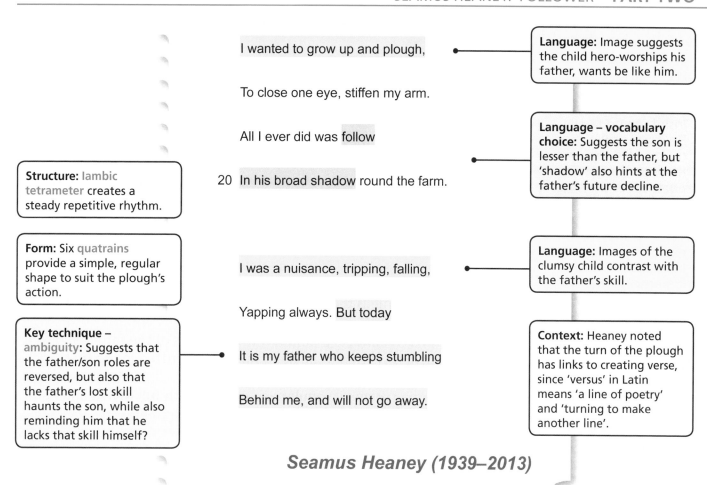

Structure: Iambic tetrameter creates a steady repetitive rhythm.

Form: Six quatrains provide a simple, regular shape to suit the plough's action.

Key technique – ambiguity: Suggests that the father/son roles are reversed, but also that the father's lost skill haunts the son, while also reminding him that he lacks that skill himself?

I wanted to grow up and plough,

To close one eye, stiffen my arm.

All I ever did was follow

20 In his broad shadow round the farm.

I was a nuisance, tripping, falling,

Yapping always. But today

It is my father who keeps stumbling

Behind me, and will not go away.

Seamus Heaney (1939–2013)

Language: Image suggests the child hero-worships his father, wants be like him.

Language – vocabulary choice: Suggests the son is lesser than the father, but 'shadow' also hints at the father's future decline.

Language: Images of the clumsy child contrast with the father's skill.

Context: Heaney noted that the turn of the plough has links to creating verse, since 'versus' in Latin means 'a line of poetry' and 'turning to make another line'.

Glossary

1 shafts = blades or sticks used to cut the earth
2 headrig = soil left at the top of field to ease the turning of the plough

KEY CONTEXT (A03)

Seamus Heaney (1939–2013) was born in Northern Ireland into a large Irish farming family. He is generally regarded as one of the most important poets of his time. He received the Nobel Prize in Literature in 1995. Heaney's own experience of the Irish rural world and in particular the connection to the soil is often present in his poetry. In 'Follower', there are several references – 'land' (10), 'ground' (11) – and some are repeated – 'furrow' (3, 12), 'sod' (7, 14), giving a subtle emphasis that helps to create a strong sense of the agricultural environment.

SUMMARY

- The son remembers his father's physical expertise as a ploughman.
- He recalls how, as a child following his father in the field, he wanted to develop the same expertise.
- The son discovers that he does not have the same talent as his father.
- Now, his father in old age is the one who stumbles and follows his son.

KEY ASPECTS OF THE POEM

A   An important theme is the **relationship** between the **father** and his **son**.

B   Another theme is the **bond** with the **soil** through the son's desire to plough the land.

C   The powerful imagery contrasts the portraits of the father and son.

D   The poem is written in six quatrains and is written in the **first person**.

E   The rhyme scheme is **regular** and created with **full rhyme** and half-rhyme, and the poem is written in iambic tetrameter.

KEY SETTING: THE WORKING RURAL ENVIRONMENT (A03)

In a complex series of images in the first verse, Heaney presents a striking portrait of the father as ploughman, a man who is at one with the land he tends and the machinery he uses. Together the horse, the plough and the father are a powerful machine in which the father's 'shoulders' (2) are between 'the shafts' (3) of the 'horse-plough' (1) and the 'furrow' (3) created. The image is also a nautical one: the father is like a great sailing ship. His 'shoulders' (2) are 'globed like a full sail strung' (2), as though ploughing the waves. The horse strains 'at his clicking tongue' (4), suggesting a machine in action. Images of machinery – 'the headrig' (8), 'the steel-pointed sock' (6), and of toil – 'the sweating team' (9) constantly remind us of work and the father's physical strength.

TOP TIP: WRITING ABOUT THE CHILD (A01)

Heaney's portrayal of the small son is of a clumsy, exuberant and demanding child. While the father is highly skilled and can map 'the furrow exactly' (12), the child follows 'In his broad shadow' (20), or sometimes he rides on his father's back to the movement of the plough. The child's adoration of his father is highlighted in the simple first line of the penultimate verse: 'I wanted to grow up and plough' (17). Not fully understanding the craft involved, he wanted, nonetheless, to emulate his father's physical strength and expertise, and perhaps, Heaney is also implying, his father's masculinity.

KEY TECHNIQUE: THE MOVEMENT OF THE PLOUGH

The poem has a regular pattern of quatrains, which seem to move with the plough up and down the land, 'Dipping and rising' (16). Heaney reinforces this effect by the frequent use of run on lines (**enjambment**). These lines not only run from one line to another, but in one instance from one verse to another, so that 'with a single pluck./Of reins' (8, 9) we feel as if we too turn with 'the sweating team' (9) to come back down the field again.

AIMING HIGH: CHANGING POSITIONS ⭐

The final lines of the poem, 'It is my father who keeps stumbling/Behind me, and will not go away' (23, 24), are critical to an understanding of the son's continuing relationship with his father. The tone of the lines suggests that just as the child was 'a nuisance' (21) pestering his father at his work, so the father, a faltering old man, pesters the son, a grown man. But there is also something deeper at work. The potency of the child's early experience and his desire to be like his father, 'An expert' (5), has not resulted in the son pursuing his father's work. By contrast, the son's lack of physical talent suggests that he remains in his father's shadow. Is he a son who did not live up to parental expectations? Does he feel his father is holding him to account? Or does he feel guilt at not choosing the same path in life? Several interpretations are possible.

REVISION FOCUS: THE RHYTHM OF THE LINE

The poem is written in iambic tetrameter and has a strong musical quality with a steady beat. Read the poem to yourself again, emphasising the rhythm. In the first line, work out which syllables are stressed and which are unstressed. Now do the same for the remaining lines of the verse. Read the poem once more, thinking about why the rhythm suits the poem. What movement do you think it reinforces?

CHECKPOINT 8

The small child's imitation of the father's skill is captured in one particular line. Which line do you think this is, and what does it reveal?

Language: A span is the gap between the thumb and little finger of a hand, when fully extended. Here, two people are needed to hold each end of the tape measure (once it exceeds the son's outstretched hands).

Key technique – double meaning: A 'single span' is only short, suggesting both the mother's need to help her son with anything more than a small task, and the speaker's irritation with this.

Viewpoint: First person, present tense. The speaker/son is addressing his mother about her help prior to his move to a new home.

Structure – enjambment: Heavily used in stanzas two and three to emphasise the tape measure unreeling as the son ascends the stairs.

Key technique – double meaning: Refers to the generation gap and the shared history between son and mother.

Language: Powerful compound word suggests an astronaut tethered to the 'mother' craft.

Key technique – colloquialism: Suggesting that the son has reached breaking point and wants freedom from his mother's control.

Structure: The structure of the poem shifts as the speaker's view changes from the confines of the attic to a panoramic view of the sky, suggesting a bid for freedom beyond his mother's control.

Language: Images of wide, open spaces, implying the **theme** of freedom, as opposed to a house interior, suggesting **confinement**.

Key technique: The tape measure becomes an extended metaphor for linking the son and mother (like an umbilical cord) and suggesting mother/son bond as a **theme**.

Language – vocabulary choice: A 'Kite' flies but is attached to a restraining string, as the mother, (an 'Anchor') restrains her son.

Form: The irregular lines reflect the irregularity of the tape unreeling as the speaker climbs to the attic.

Sound – assonance: Short 'i' reinforces the mother's attempt to cling on to the tape measure and her son.

Mother, any distance

Mother, any distance greater than a single span

requires a second pair of hands.

You come to help me measure windows, pelmets, doors,

the acres of the walls, the prairies of the floors.

5   You at the zero-end, me with the spool of tape, recording

length, reporting metres, centimetres back to base, then leaving

up the stairs, the line still feeding out, unreeling

years between us. Anchor. Kite.

I space-walk through the empty bedrooms, climb

10   the ladder to the loft, to breaking point, where something

has to give;

two floors below your fingertips still pinch

the last one-hundredth of an inch ... I reach

towards a hatch that opens on an endless sky

15   to fall or fly.

Sound – alliteration: The soft 'f' sound reinforces the idea of flight.

Simon Armitage (1963–)

Key technique – ambiguity: Does the son think his bid for freedom will succeed, or does he still need his mother?

Context: The poem comes from *The Book of Matches* (1993) and should take no longer to read than it does to strike a match and let it burn.

SUMMARY

- The speaker is visiting a new home into which he has not yet moved.
- His mother is helping him take measurements around the house.
- He goes upstairs and walks through the empty bedrooms, while his mother continues measuring on the floor below.
- He reaches the loft and opens the skylight.

KEY ASPECTS OF THE POEM

- **A** The main theme is **the mother/son bond and the need for separation**. Other themes include **freedom and restriction**.
- **B** The poem has end rhymes and internal rhymes.
- **C** The **rhythm** is **irregular** and enjambment is frequently used.
- **D** The poem is written in the **first person** and is addressed to the mother.

KEY SETTING: MOVING AWAY **A01**

The setting focuses on the move to a new home, a two-storey house with a loft. The house is empty of furniture, perhaps representing a fresh start, away from the parental home. The speaker's mother is helping him 'measure windows, pelmets, doors,/the acres of the walls' (3, 4) in preparation for filling the space. She holds one end of a measuring tape, while he holds the other. He climbs the ladder that leads to a loft, still holding the now taut measuring tape and aware that his mother is connected to him beneath, and still fussily measuring. In the loft there is a 'hatch' that opens 'on an endless sky' (14) that seems to be outside the confines of his mother's control.

KEY TECHNIQUE: MULTI-LAYERED METAPHOR **A02**

The poet uses the measuring tape as an **extended metaphor** of connection. As the speaker 'space-walk[s]' (9) through the bedroom with the measuring tape we see an image of an astronaut tethered to the spacecraft (the 'mother' ship). The metaphor occurs again with the mention of 'Anchor. Kite' (8). While a kite may appear to soar, a string controls it. The mother represents the anchor restraining her son; the kite, his attempts to 'fly' (15), to free himself from her. It is also possible to see the metaphor as the umbilical cord. So the 'breaking point' (10) is a **metaphor** of separation, the point at which the speaker feels he must disconnect and forge his own life.

KEY QUOTATION: A BID FOR FREEDOM? **A01**

The speaker, though acutely aware of the restrictions his mother places on him, seems uncertain that his bid for freedom will succeed. The final lines might have ended with the speaker opening the skylight 'on an endless sky/... to fly' (14, 15) so that he imagines himself free of his mother's constraints. Instead, the last line reads: 'to fall or fly' (15). The reader wonders whether the speaker has the determination to break free.

KEY STRUCTURE: THE SPOOL OF TAPE **A02**

The poet frequently uses enjambment. The effect is to conjure up an **image** of the speaker 'with the spool of tape, recording/length' (5, 6), with the tape running behind him as he climbs to other floors. In addition, the irregularity of the lines mirrors the trail of the measuring tape, until in the last verse we have a sudden halt, a **caesura** 'where something/has to give' (10, 11). The tape becomes so stretched it can no longer unreel. This also suggests the tension that exists between mother and son.

CHECKPOINT 9 **A01**

Why do you think the poet chose the title 'Mother, any distance'?

TOP TIP **A02**

At the end of the poem, the mother's 'fingertips still pinch/the last one-hundredth of an inch' (12, 13) as she holds the very end of the measuring tape. We might also feel she is clinging to it, unwilling to release it. Reread the last verse and decide how it is a metaphor for her attitude to her son.

TOP TIP: WRITING ABOUT DOUBLE MEANINGS **A01**

Notice how the poet uses the measuring tape unwinding to create the image 'unreeling/years between us' (7, 8). At first reading, this appears to refer to the generation gap, the difference in lifestyle or values that exists between mother and son and which alienates the speaker from his mother. However, the image could also refer to the period of time that the speaker shared with his mother when he was a child. This shared history binds them together, just as the measuring tape connects them. Rather than thinking that the meaning is **ambiguous**, we can think of it as having a double meaning that reflects the speaker's confused relationship with his mother.

Structure: The speaker is an omniscient/all-seeing speaker, able to shift position in time from 'before [she] was born' (line 19) to her childhood years (line 12) and also to the present ('and now', line 13).

Language: The image suggests a rotating glitterball, or the dancers' excited eyes on the crowded floor.

Key technique – repetition: Shows the sense of ownership the child feels over the mother, reinforcing the idea that having a child dominates a mother's life.

Sound – alliteration: Repetition of 'h' and 'r' reinforces the bouncy rhythm to help conjure a childhood memory of excitement and dressing up.

Theme: The intense sight-smell image of the mother suggests the daughter's love for her.

Language: The image suggests dancing on the pavement and also the Hollywood 'Walk of Fame' with its named stars, further reinforcing the idea of glamour.

Language: The image suggests the speaker may be looking at a photograph.

Context: The 1950s star Marilyn Monroe. Suggests her famous pose with her dress billowing up as she stood over a subway grate, reinforcing the idea of glamour.

Key technique – metaphor: For romantic possibilities and cinema dates ('fizzy' suggests sparkling wine).

Key technique – enjambment: Reflecting the way the speaker imagines her mother must have danced.

Key technique – caesura: Emphasises the young woman's carefree attitude.

Language: 'relics' suggests the loss of the speaker's younger self, as well as the mother's.

Language: The image suggests the sound of high heels on the pavement and a ghost's chains, reinforcing the idea of the mother's past life and death.

Structure: The image takes us back to the beginning of the poem and the title, reminding us that in the photograph the mother will always be young and glamorous, before the speaker was born.

Context: Scottish context.

Before You Were Mine

I'm ten years away from the corner you laugh on

with your pals, Maggie McGeeney and Jean Duff.

The three of you bend from the waist, holding

each other, or your knees, and shriek at the pavement.

5   Your polka-dot dress blows round your legs. Marilyn.

I'm not here yet. The thought of me doesn't occur

in the ballroom with the thousand eyes, the fizzy, movie tomorrows

the right walk home could bring. I knew you would dance

like that. Before you were mine, your Ma stands at the close

10   with a hiding for the late one. You reckon it's worth it.

The decade ahead of my loud, possessive yell was the best one, eh?

I remember my hands in those high-heeled red shoes, relics,

and now your ghost clatters toward me over George Square

till I see you, clear as scent, under the tree,

15   with its lights, and whose small bites on your neck, sweetheart?

Cha cha cha! You'd teach me the steps on the way home from Mass,

stamping stars from the wrong pavement. Even then

I wanted the bold girl winking in Portobello, somewhere

in Scotland, before I was born. That glamorous love lasts

20   where you sparkle and waltz and laugh before you were mine.

Carol Ann Duffy (1955–)

SUMMARY

- The speaker imagines what her mother's life was like ten years before the speaker was born. She sees her as a teenager with few responsibilities and the freedom to enjoy her life.
- In the first verse she may be looking at a photograph of her mother laughing with friends.
- There is a touch of glamour in the way her mother dresses.
- She pictures her mother dancing at a local ballroom and going to the cinema.
- The speaker also recalls memories from her own childhood that hint at her mother's life as a younger woman, such as holding her high-heeled shoes or her mother teaching her to dance.

KEY CONTEXT (A03)

Carol Ann Duffy (b. 1955) became Poet Laureate in 2009. Her poetry is usually concerned with women's experience and she also writes plays, as well as stories and poems for children. Duffy often draws on popular icons and historical figures or sources. The famous photo of 'Marilyn' (5) Monroe (though not wearing a polka dot dress) standing above a subway grating was taken in 1954. The image, recreated in the poem, helps to conjure up the period and **mood**.

KEY ASPECTS OF THE POEM

A   The main theme is **the daughter's love for her mother**. Other themes are **change**, **loss** and **personal history**.

B   It is a free verse poem with an **irregular rhythm** and a little internal rhyme.

C   The poem uses alliteration and assonance.

D   It is written in five quintains in the **first person**, and is addressed to the mother at a time before the speaker was born.

KEY SETTING: MOVING AWAY (A01)

The poem opens with an affectionate depiction of the speaker's mother and two friends, laughing on a street corner. An image of Marilyn Monroe, the famous 1950s Hollywood star, is referenced, as the speaker visualises her own spirited mother and her 'pals' (2) imitating a famous pose. Since the first verse includes specific visual details of the people and events, it suggests that the speaker is looking at a photograph, or is imagining doing so. The setting of the poem is Scotland. 'George Square' (13) is one of Glasgow's public thoroughfares, while 'Portobello' (18) is a district of Edinburgh. In the speaker's mind the imagined cities are ones of youthful excitement, vibrant with nightlife and possibility. The ballroom's 'thousand eyes' (7) seem to be the ceiling lights or the glitter ball that rotates in the centre, or perhaps the eyes of the dancers. The 'fizzy, movie tomorrows' (7) hint at romance; at the prospect of being invited on a date, of finding love.

TOP TIP (A01)

Notice how in the third verse we are brought into the present through a striking **image**. The speaker sees her mother as a ghost that 'clatters toward' (13) her. The clattering noise has associations with the 'high-heeled red shoes' (12), but also with the clatter of a ghost's chains. We could interpret this as the ghost of youth. It brings with it a heightened depiction for the speaker, but also a sense of loss, hinting at the speaker's own memories from childhood – 'relics' (12) – as well as her mother's lost youth.

EXAM FOCUS: WRITING ABOUT EFFECTS   (A02)

You may be asked to write about memorable images in the poem. Read what one student has written.

> Duffy creates many images in the poem that appeal to the sense of sight, but the most startling image is when the daughter sees her mother 'clear as scent'. It appeals both to the sense of sight and smell, and the effect is to remind us of the way a powerful smell can bring back a memory especially vividly. Similarly, 'stamping stars' suggests the sense of sound and touch as the feet hit the pavement when the daughter and mother dance the cha-cha. It also reminds us of the Hollywood Walk of Fame. The sibilant in the image further adds a hiss of fire, as though real stars were being branded on the ground.

A good example of how the poet has achieved her effects, and what these are

A useful connective to highlight a parallel point

A good example of a technique and its effect

Now you try it:

Add a sentence that shows how another image evokes the sense of sight especially vividly.

KEY QUOTATION: THE ELUSIVE PICTURE   (A01)

'Even then/I wanted the bold girl winking in Portobello' (19, 20) implies that the speaker's teenage years were less exciting than the mother's. However, the image creates another effect. It suggests the fascination children often have with their parents' early lives – as though they can piece together a jigsaw of their past to obtain a complete picture. But, like glamour, such a picture is elusive. It only exists in the imagination, as it does in the poem.

KEY VOICE: FROM THE FUTURE   (A02)

The speaker addresses the mother from a state before birth, but also shifts to recall her own childhood memories. The voice the poet chooses is an adult voice. It fondly identifies with the teenage depiction of the mother, by using **colloquialism**, as in the reference to 'The decade ahead … was the best one, eh?' (11) but it is not the voice of a child or teenager, which would sound less experienced. The voice also has a possessive quality. It speaks to the mother as a mother would to a child. For example, we might expect a daughter, whatever her age, to say: *Before I was yours*, deferring to the mother. Instead we have 'Before You Were Mine' as the title, which is repeated in the poem and gives a sense of ownership. It reinforces the idea that having children dominates a mother's life. The daughter is aware that through her birth and 'loud, possessive yell' (11) her mother has lost her freedom and that the previous 'decade' was indeed the 'best' (11).

CHECKPOINT 10   (A01)

Apart from a sense of possession, what other **connotations** does the title 'Before You Were Mine' have?

Key technique – pathetic fallacy: The clouds are given the human trait of determination.

Language/Form: Extreme weather followed by a 'break' (also shown in the line break) suggests a quarrel followed by a pause in the dispute.

Viewpoint: First person past tense. The speaker addresses his lover as they walk around a lake after the rain.

Winter Swans

The clouds had given their all –

two days of rain and then a break

in which we walked,

Form: The tercets move easily from one to another, helped by frequent enjambment suggesting the walk around the lake.

Language: Image suggests the couple's relationship is mired, like the earth.

the waterlogged earth

5   gulping for breath at our feet

as we skirted the lake, silent and apart,

Language: Nature imagery; the swans' pairing is a reminder of commitment in a relationship.

until the swans came and stopped us

with a show of tipping in unison. [6]

As if rolling weights down their bodies to their heads

Language: Imagery suggests that the relationship is struggling to survive and reinforces the separation between the couple.

Language: Pairing is a common feature throughout the poem to emphasise the couple's relationship (see lines 2, 13, 17, 20).

Language: 'iceberg' suggests coldness and 'feather' softness, reflecting opposing aspects of the couple's relationship.

10   they halved themselves in the dark water,

icebergs of white feather, paused before returning again

like boats righting in rough weather.

Key technique – simile: Shows that the difficulties ('rough weather') in the relationship can be mended ('righted').

Language: Comment meant to reflect on speaker's own relationship.

'They mate for life' you said as they left,

porcelain over the **stilling** water. I didn't reply

15   but as we moved on through the afternoon light,

Language: 'stilling' suggests a calming of the dispute.

Language – metaphor: Porcelain is white, (suggesting marriage) but also easily broken, suggesting that care and respect should be features of a relationship.

Sound – sibilant: Helps create a softer, gentler **mood** as the couple move towards reconciliation.

slow-**s**tepping in the lake's **s**hingle and **s**and,

I noticed our hands, that had, somehow,

swum the distance between us

Language: Image of the couple holding hands, reminiscent of the swan's movement.

Key technique – simile: Compares the holding of hands with the folding of wings.

and folded, one over the other,

20   like a pair of wings settling after flight.

Owen Sheers (1974–)

Form/Context: The final couplet provides a resolution (as it does in a sonnet/ love poem) to the separation.

Key technique: Repeated images of the swans become a **motif** that reinforces the **theme** of **love and reconciliation.**

SUMMARY

- The speaker recalls a walk with his partner around a lake after rain.
- The track around the lake is saturated and difficult to walk on.
- As they walk two swans arrive and land on the lake together, dip and swim.
- The couple stop to watch the swan's display.
- The swans leave and the speaker's partner notes that swans stay together until one dies.
- The speaker and his partner are reconciled.

KEY ASPECTS OF THE POEM

A   The main theme is **reconciliation**. Other themes are **commitment** and the **natural world**.

B   The poem is free verse with some **rhyme**.

C   The images evoke the **natural world** and **intensity of feeling**. The poem contains an important motif.

D   The poet also uses **pathetic fallacy** to describe aspects of nature.

E   The poem is written in six **tercets** with a **couplet** at the end. **Enjambment** is frequently used.

F   The poem is told in the **first person** and can be read as addressed to the partner or the reader.

KEY SETTING: THE LAKESIDE   **A01**

The poet has chosen a lakeside after heavy rain as a setting. A couple circle the lake treading on 'the waterlogged earth/gulping for breath' (4, 5), which alludes both to their squelching feet and the way their relationship seems stuck as a result of unresolved problems. The profusion of water reinforces these implications. Heavy rain, in which 'The clouds had given their all' (1) implies extreme weather, if not a storm, and again suggests the couple have been through difficulties in their relationship. As they walk they are 'silent' (6), much like a lake after turbulence. A still lake can signal hidden depths beneath a deceptive calm. Only when the two swans appear does the lake respond and change.

AIMING HIGH: THE SWANS ⭐

For a more developed response you could focus on how the imagery of the swans dominates. The couple are mired by their differences and the **tone** is bleak 'until the swans' (7) arrive. Unlike the couple, the swans are together. They dip 'in unison' (8) then bob up again in the water 'like boats righting in rough weather' (12). The **simile** shows what can be mended between the speaker and his partner. In other words, the 'rough weather' in the relationship can be overcome. Affected by the swans' display, the partner breaks the silence by noting that swans 'mate for life' (13). This is the broader perspective needed to remind the couple of their commitment to each other. The poet uses another simile to allude to the swans again. The simple gesture of holding hands 'like a pair of wings settling after flight' (20) brings the couple together. The various images of the birds throughout the poem form a **motif** that reinforces the theme of reconciliation. Now consider how this motif shifts the tone of the poem.

TOP TIP (A01)

Compare the different **alliteration** in the first and the last verse (including the sixth tercet). Think about the effect the poet creates, and how this relates to the tone and meaning of the poem.

KEY QUOTATION: HOLDING HANDS (A01)

'I noticed our hands, that had, somehow,/swum the distance between us' (17, 18) is an important image. The word 'swum' has clear associations with the swans swimming on the lake, and the poet is signalling that the swans have made a subtle impact on the unhappy relationship. Without realising quite how, the couple are holding hands. Notice also how the **sibilant** is frequently used. It occurs as soft 'c' as well as 's'. Consider the quality of the sound and the effect the poet creates at this point in the poem.

CHECKPOINT 11 (A01)

What features and images in the poem can you find that reinforce the idea of a couple, and why?

TOP TIP: WRITING ABOUT CLOSURE (A02)

The poet has chosen to end with a **couplet**, which is often used to bring closure to a poem. A **sonnet**, also a love poem, ends with a couplet. Here it can represent the speaker and his partner. The effect is to imply that, like the couplet, the two are a couple again. Note how 'flight' (20) rhymes with 'light' (15), which also creates closure as well as a sense of partnership, reinforcing that the difficulties between the two are ended. The meaning of the noun 'light' further suggests that the darkness in the relationship has been dispelled. Remember too, that 'flight' is accompanied by 'after' to read 'after flight' (20). Decide what this suggests.

Key technique – pun: 'Singh' is the surname of all Sikh men; 'sing-song' is slang for a voice that has a marked cadence and is a negative stereotype.

Context: The poem uses the accent of English speakers whose first language is Punjabi, (e.g. 'ov' meaning 'of' and 'vee' meaning 'we').

Key technique: Frequent repetition emphasises the musical quality of the speaker's voice.

Form: The stanzas and lines are laid out in an erratic fashion, reflecting the way the speaker runs his shop.

Key technique – rhyme: Helps the rise and fall of the voice and the poem's musicality.

Form/Sound – chorus: A lively, rocking cadence that reminds us of the poem's title and its meaning.

Key technique – double meaning: 'mouse' refers to the computer device; the saying 'playing cat and mouse' means teasing.

Key technique – metaphor: Draws on the vivid colours of the Punjab region to accentuate the wife's colourful swearing.

Language: Suggests the bride has a contrasting nature, both hard ('gun') and soft ('teddy').

Singh Song!

I run just one **ov** my daddy's shops

from 9 o'clock to 9 o'clock

and he vunt me not to hav a break

but ven nobody in, I do di lock –

5   cos up di stairs is my **newly bride**

vee share in chapatti

vee share in di chutney

after vee hav made luv

like vee rowing through Putney –

10   Ven I return vid my pinnie untied

di shoppers always point and cry:

*Hey **Singh**, ver yoo **bin**?*

Yor lemons are limes

yor bananas are plantain,

15   *dis dirty little floor need a little bit of mop*

in di worst Indian shop

on di whole Indian road –

Above my head high heel tap di ground

as my vife on di web is playing wid di mouse

20   ven she netting two cat on her Sikh lover site

she book dem for di meat at di cheese ov her price –

my bride

she effing at my mum

in all di colours of Punjabi

25   den stumble like a drunk

making fun at my daddy

my bride

tiny eyes ov a gun

and di tummy ov a teddy

Key technique – irony: *Singh Song!* challenges the stereotype of English/Punjabi speakers by taking possession of the insult and mocking it.

Language: Challenges the stereotype of the obedient, hardworking Asian son who runs a corner shop.

Viewpoint: First person present tense. The speaker tells of his love for his wife.

Theme: 'bride' suggests a new **marriage** and **romantic love**.

Voice: Uses an English idiom, making the speaker believable.

Voice: Line ends on an upward note, creating a vibrant, cheerful mood.

Key technique – ambiguity: Suggests the wife is making contact with two men, challenging the stereotype of the submissive Asian wife?

Language: The wife's behaviour challenges the stereotype of the obedient Asian bride.

Language: The wife's dress style is multicultural: 'Punk' hairstyle, Scottish tartan and working man's jacket challenge the stereotype of the Asian wife.

30 my bride

she hav a red crew cut

and she wear a Tartan sari

a donkey jacket and some pumps

on di squeak ov di girls dat are pinching my sweeties –

Language: Suggests love play and the speaker's affection for his wife.

35 Ven I return from di tickle ov my bride

di shoppers always point and cry:

Hey Singh, ver yoo bin?

Di milk is out ov date

and di bread is alvays stale,

Key technique: Extends the bouncy rhythm to create a comic effect as the chorus criticises the speaker for his poor management.

40 *di tings yoo hav on offer yoo hav never got in stock*

in di worst Indian shop

on di whole Indian road –

Structure: Pace slows to reflect the mysterious, secretive night.

Late in di midnight hour

ven yoo shoppers are wrap up quiet

45 ven di precinct is **c**oncrete-**c**ool

Key technique – alliteration: 'c' of 'cool' suggests the opposite, accentuates the image of a hot summer night and romantic passion.

vee cum down whi**s**pering **s**tair**s**

Sound: The sibilant creates a playful, romantic mood.

and **s**it on my **s**ilver **s**tool,

from behind di chocolate bars

vee stare past di half-price window signs

50 at di beaches ov di UK in di brightey moon –

Key technique: Universal symbol of love.

Form – couplets: Often used for love poems and suited to the poem's theme.

from di stool each night she say,

How much do yoo charge for dat moon baby?

from di stool each night I say,

Is half di cost ov yoo baby,

Context: The ghazal, an Eastern love poem, explores how love may not be equally felt. Are the wife's feelings for her husband as sincere as his?

from di stool each night she say,

55 *How much does dat come to baby?*

Structure: Rhyme and rhythm are irregular, supporting the erratic form.

from di stool each night I say,

Is priceless baby –

Daljit Nagra (1966–)

SUMMARY

- A young man, who is the speaker, runs one of his father's grocery shops and is expected to work hard.
- He is newly married and he and his bride live above the shop.
- He neglects the shop and regularly slips away to make love to his wife and share Asian food.
- The shoppers complain that his shop is not well kept.
- His wife, meanwhile, is on her computer. She is a strong-minded woman who pursues her own activities.
- Late at night the couple sneak down to the shop to stare at the moon.

KEY ASPECTS OF THE POEM

A The main theme is **marriage**. Other themes are **romance** and **identity**.

B The poem is largely a **comic love poem** in which some ambiguity is used.

C **Repetition** is a key feature of the language, and there is a chorus. The **rhyme** and **rhythm** is **irregular**.

D The poem is written in **phonetic language**, in the **first person**.

KEY SETTING: THE SHOP **A01**

As a setting, the poet uses a grocer's shop run by the speaker, a British Asian. He sells a variety of food from 'lemons' (13) and 'bananas' (14) to 'chocolate bars' (48). However, he ignores his father's wishes and does as he pleases, implying that he has little interest in the business. The shop is in poor condition because he neglects it, even when the customers point out that 'Di milk is out ov date' (38) and 'di bread is alvays stale' (39). He has other interests and would rather close the shop from time to time during the day and slip upstairs to the flat above to make love to his 'newly bride' (5).

KEY VOICE: MUSICALITY **A02**

The poet creates a highly musical voice. Listen to the upward sound of 'cry' in 'di shoppers always point and cry' (11) and the rise and fall created by the internal rhyme of 'Singh' and 'bin' in *'Hey Singh, ver yoo bin?'* (12). The speaker is an English-speaking first-generation immigrant, whose mother tongue is Punjabi. To create an authentic **voice** the poet has used phonetic spelling that communicates easily and is often repeated: 'v' frequently replaces 'w' to read 'he vunt me' (3) or 'vee' as in 'vee share in' (6, 7). Similarly the letter 'd' replaces 'th'. The overall effect of these techniques is to create a voice that is vibrant, optimistic and joyous, reflecting the speaker's love for his new bride.

KEY CONTEXT **A03**

Daljit Nagra (b. 1966) was born in London. He is of Sikh Punjabi descent. He won the Forward Poetry Prize (2007) for his first collection. Some of his poetry, such as 'Singh Song!' challenges stereotypes of British Asians – for instance, the assumption held by some that all British Asians conform to a traditional Indian culture.

TOP TIP: WRITING ABOUT MUSICALITY   **A02**

One of the main features of the poem is its **chorus**, which by its nature depends on repetition. The shoppers' comments, such as 'dis dirty little floor need a little bit of mop' (15), are reported in a lively, **dipodic** manner, suited to a chorus and referencing the poem's title. However, Daljit Nagra shapes the other verses in an erratic fashion. Verses and lines are of different lengths and the rhyme occurs irregularly. They mirror the way the speaker runs his shop – closing sporadically 'ven nobody in' (4) so he can visit his bride. Structurally, there is a slowing of the pace towards the end, appropriately 'in di midnight hour' (43); the effect is contemplative. The speaker regards his urban life and a softer romantic **tone** follows as the husband and bride engage in an affectionate tête-à-tête.

KEY TECHNIQUE: CAT AND MOUSE   **A02**

The poet presents the bride as playful and romantic, if money conscious, as she jokes in the last verses, but he also sounds a more hard-headed note when the bride visits her 'Sikh lover' (20) website. Here, ambiguity arises around 'mouse' (19) and 'cat' (20); 'playing wid di mouse' (19) suggests not only the computer device, but the **idiom** 'cat and mouse', meaning to toy with or tease. It implies that she is the cat teasing the men – the mice – on the website. However, the wife is also 'netting two cat' (20), or catching two young men at a bargain – 'di cheese ov her price' (21); in other words, on her own terms. Whatever the interpretation, the effect is much the same: it implies extramarital relations. The suggestion, therefore, is that the speaker and his wife have an open relationship, since he expresses no objection to his bride's behaviour. The relationship challenges the stereotypical view of an Asian marriage, which assumes a passive wife under her husband's control. The poet could be making the point that whoever we are, we lead unique lives and should be acknowledged as individuals.

CHECKPOINT 12   **A01**

How is the speaker's father different from his son? What effect do you think the poet wants to achieve?

TOP TIP: REQUITED LOVE?   **A02**

The ghazal, a traditional form of love poetry from India and Persia, is written in couplets and deals with unattainable love, or love in which the loved one is less than sincere. Study the couplets at the end of 'Singh Song!' in which the speaker reports his bride's questions. Consider whether or not the speaker's love is requited. Is his wife's love sincere? Does he love his wife more than she loves him?

REVISION FOCUS: THE BRIDE

Reread lines 22–34, from 'my bride' to '… pinching my sweeties'. Draw a spider diagram. Note all the features and quotations that denote the bride's appearance. In the same way, add notes and quotations that describe her behaviour. What effect has the poet created? Write a short commentary that describes the bride, selecting quotations to support what you say.

Viewpoint: The first person speaker, a grandson, explores the nature of his grandfather by imagining how he would climb up him.

Theme: The climb may be dangerous, bringing back upsetting memories when remembering his grandfather, suggesting **memory** as a **theme**.

Structure: The climb/exploration of memory begins energetically, at the grandfather's feet/foot of a mountain.

Context: Waterhouse had a special knowledge of landscape, which is reflected in the landforms mentioned.

Key technique – oxymoron: The contradiction suggests that though the grandfather is dead, he is kept alive through the speaker's love.

Language: Suggests a childhood memory of the grandfather's reliability and strength.

Language: Suggests there was affection between the speaker and his grandfather

Sound – sibilant: The soft 's' enhances the gentle exploration of the grandfather's eyes, searching for who he is.

Structure – resolution: The exhausted climber has achieved his goal, and has become closer to his grandfather through searching his memory.

Language: Suggests the grandfather worked outside or cared little about his appearance.

Key technique – metaphor: Suggests both the 'grip' on the mountain and an attempt to recover an image of the grandfather, suggesting **childhood** as a **theme**.

Language: Helps to build a picture of the grandfather as working on the land.

Language: 'gently' reveals the speaker's care and respect for his grandfather.

Key technique – extended metaphor: The grandfather is compared to a mountain and its features throughout the poem (e.g. 'scar').

Language: Suggests there are dangers in recalling memories, reinforces line 4.

Language: Reminds us of children's fascination with faces.

Theme: Conveys the strong **love** felt for the grandfather.

Climbing My Grandfather

I decide to do it free, without a rope or net.
First, the old brogues, dusty and cracked;
an easy scramble onto his trousers,
pushing into the weave, trying to get a grip.
5 By the overhanging[1] shirt I change
direction, traverse along his belt[2]
to an earth-stained hand. The nails
are splintered and give good purchase,
the skin of his finger is smooth and thick
10 like warm ice. On his arm I discover
the glassy ridge of a scar,[3] place my feet
gently in the old stitches and move on.
At his still firm shoulder, I rest for a while
in the shade, not looking down,
15 for climbing has its dangers, then pull
myself up the loose skin of his neck
to a smiling mouth to drink among teeth.
Refreshed, I cross the screed[4] cheek,
to stare into his brown eyes, watch a pupil
20 slowly open and close. Then up over
the forehead, the wrinkles well-spaced
and easy, to his thick hair (soft and white
at this altitude), reaching for the summit,
where gasping for breath I can only lie
25 watching clouds and birds circle,
feeling his heat, knowing
the slow pulse of his good heart.

Andrew Waterhouse (1958–2001)

Glossary

[1] overhanging = jutting rock formation
[2] scar = a bare, protruding rocky place
[3] belt = a group of mountain ranges
[4] screed = a level layer

SUMMARY

- A grandson imagines himself climbing up his grandfather from his feet to the top of his head.
- He sees himself as a mountaineer.
- We have a detailed description of his grandfather's clothes and features as an elderly man.
- Once the speaker reaches the shoulders he rests and takes a drink.
- Then he proceeds to the summit, where he lies exhausted, staring above him.

KEY ASPECTS OF THE POEM

A   The main theme is **family memory**, in this case of a grandfather. Other themes include **achievement**, **mountaineering** and **childhood**.

B   It is a free verse poem that is also a narrative told as a **journey**.

C   Enjambment and caesura are frequently used.

D   The poem is an extended metaphor and also includes related images.

E   It is told in the **first person**.

KEY SETTING: THE MOUNTAIN (A02)

Most adults seem gigantic to children, and men in particular do, so the idea that the grandfather is a mountain seems apt. This becomes an extended metaphor: 'the glassy ridge of a scar' (11) on the grandfather's arm is a place on the mountain for the climber to 'place' his 'feet' (11) and the 'still firm shoulder' (13) is a place to rest.

TOP TIP: WRITING ABOUT THE JOURNEY (A01)

The poem is told as a journey; one that a mountaineer would take. Each stage is signalled. For example, the simple connective 'First' (2) begins the climb. These signals help to give the poem its pattern. When the climber reaches the summit, there is relief. The speaker has reached his goal, literally in reaching the summit and metaphorically in getting closer to his grandfather, and perhaps himself.

EXAM FOCUS: WRITING ABOUT EFFECTS (A02)

Read what one student has written about the how the poet creates character.

> The poet creates effects through the extended metaphor of the mountain that suggests what the grandfather was like, and there are several examples of his appearance, which suggest his character. His 'brogues' are 'dusty and cracked', implying he did not care much about his appearance, or more likely that he worked outdoors, suggested by his 'earth-stained hand' and 'splintered nails'. He also has a 'firm shoulder' where the climber can rest. The word 'firm' implies that he is still strong and steady for an elderly man and also that his character is steady and reliable. At the end of the poem the climber feels the old man's 'heat' and knows that his heart is 'good'. Consequently, the reader can assume that the grandfather was not only warm and honest, but that the speaker cared for him.

A strong opening that refers to a literary technique and its purpose

A good example that shows effects, and that more than one interpretation has been considered from the evidence

Connective linking cause and effect

Now you try it:

Add a final sentence to explain what the choice of a mountain tells us about the grandfather.

KEY VOICE: THE MOUNTAINEER (A02)

The **voice** is familiar in tone; that of a storyteller. It is also the voice of the mountaineer, someone who chooses an arduous and dangerous task, performed 'without a rope or net' (1). The effect is to suggest that the speaker needs to search his mind for memories of his grandfather to create him afresh. The need to be close to him is also implied in the final lines, when the speaker is in touch with 'the slow pulse of his good heart' (27). There is some ambiguity about the reason for this need. Is the memory difficult to piece together because the loss of his grandfather is so painful, or because he did not know him well enough? Or is the speaker searching for his own identity through his grandfather?

CHECKPOINT 13 (A01)

The speaker addresses the reader in the first person present tense. What effect do you think this creates?

PROGRESS AND REVISION CHECK

SECTION ONE: CHECK YOUR KNOWLEDGE

Answer these quick questions to test your basic knowledge of the poems.

1. In which poem do the lovers part in 'The dew of the morning' (9)?
2. In 'Porphyria's Lover', name two landscape features outside the cottage.
3. What activity is the boy involved in, in 'Walking Away'?
4. Who are the two friends mentioned in 'Before You Were Mine'?
5. Who was always 'Yapping' (22) in 'Follower'?
6. In what poem is the 'precinct' 'concrete-cool' (45)?
7. In 'Love's Philosophy' what do the 'winds of Heaven' (3) mix with?
8. In which poem is there a dog? What breed is it, and what is its name?
9. In which poem is the lover referred to as a 'palm-tree' (5)?
10. What type of tree is mentioned in 'Neutral Tones'?
11. Where do the speaker and his partner walk in 'Winter Swans'?
12. Name two geographical features in 'Climbing My Grandfather'.
13. What season and month are mentioned in 'Letters from Yorkshire'?
14. In which poem is there 'a second pair of hands' (2), and to whom does it refer?
15. In 'The Farmer's Bride', where did the farmer catch his wife after she ran away?
16. Who travelled through 'wind and rain' (30) to her lover?
17. In which poem is a famous person mentioned, and who is it?
18. How long ago does the speaker place the memory of the football game in 'Walking Away'?
19. In which poem does 'a pond edged with greyish leaves' (16) appear?
20. In 'The Farmer's Bride', to what animals is the wife compared? Why?

SECTION TWO: CHECK YOUR UNDERSTANDING

Here are two tasks about the significance of certain moments in two poems. These require more thought and longer responses. In each case, try to write at least three to four paragraphs.

Task 1: How does Browning present the murder in 'Porphyria's Lover', and why do you think the reader is so unprepared for the shocking events? Think about:

- The effect that Browning wished to create
- The speaker's attitude towards Porphyria before the murder

Task 2: How does Seamus Heaney convey the motion of the ploughman and his plough in the poem 'Follower'? Think about:

- The structure, rhythm and rhyme of the poem
- How these create effects

PROGRESS CHECK

GOOD PROGRESS

I can:

- Understand how each poem has a different voice or viewpoint and ideas to express. ☐
- Select well-chosen evidence, including key quotations, to support my ideas. ☐

EXCELLENT PROGRESS

I can:

- Analyse how the poets have used a range of techniques to create voices and convey ideas. ☐
- Draw on a range of carefully selected key evidence, including quotations, to support my ideas. ☐

Family ties

- 'Eden Rock': A son imagines being reunited with his parents after death.

- 'Follower': A son's admiration of his father, 'An expert' (5) ploughman.

- 'Climbing My Grandfather': A grandson explores the nature of his grandfather.

THEMES

THEME: FAMILY TIES

- The poems in the cluster cover a range of family ties from relationships within the nuclear family, with the focus on parents and children, and in one case a relationship with a grandparent in 'Climbing My Grandfather'.

- The voice and point of view is almost exclusively the son's or daughter's. The exception is 'Walking Away'. Here Cecil Day Lewis presents a father's point of view; he knows that both he and his young son must deal with separation and the 'letting go' (20) that comes with a new phase of life.

EXAM FOCUS: WRITING ABOUT EFFECTS (A02)

Read what one student has written about the theme of the father and son relationship in 'Follower' by Seamus Heaney.

> Heaney presents the son as a small boy who admired his father's skill with the horse-plough so much that he also wanted to 'grow up and plough'. He noted his father's gestures as he followed him round the field, believing that all he had to do to succeed was 'close one eye' and 'stiffen' his 'arm'. The effect created shows the child's simplicity and lack of understanding about the skill involved. Most importantly, it foreshadows the son as a man who is unable and possibly unwilling to follow in his father's footsteps.

Shows how Heaney creates effects

Qualifier that shows what you think but can't be certain about.

A good example of a literary technique that hints at future events

Now you try it:

Write a follow-on paragraph to show how the relationship between the father and son changes when the son becomes a man.

REVISION FOCUS: THEMES AND THEIR IMPORTANCE

Reread 'Climbing My Grandfather', then draw a pyramid and separate it horizontally into four parts. Decide which is the most important theme in the poem, and write it in the top section of the pyramid. Add a quotation (or more than one if you wish) to support your choice of theme. Now decide what other themes are in the poem and write them in the sections below, with suitable quotations. Rank the themes in importance, from the top down. Remember, the poem is open to interpretation. Can you find other themes that have not been suggested to you before? However, you must find quotations to support them.

'BEFORE YOU WERE MINE'

- The mother–daughter relationship is explored in 'Before You Were Mine' from the unusual perspective of the daughter before birth.
- The main theme is mother love of a type that is affectionate but also possessive, which is reflected in the title.
- There is also an implication that the adult speaker is trying to live indirectly through the mother's early experience, as though her own life lacked the 'fizzy' (7) appeal her mother's once had.
- The experience of living through the mother is particularly evident in the speaker's memories of childhood when she held 'those high-heeled red shoes' (12) and when she sees her mother as a young woman 'clear as scent' (14).
- The speaker seems to feel the need to be excessively close to her mother's early life, from which she was inevitably separate, shut out.

'MOTHER, ANY DISTANCE'

- In Simon Armitage's poem, 'Mother, any distance' the relationship between mother and son is strained.
- The theme is the struggle for separation from the parent.
- From the first verse and the mention of the jobs at the new home, measuring 'windows, pelmets, doors' (3) and so on, we know from the tedious list and the weary tone of the voice that the speaker's heart is not in the work.
- The mother, we suspect, is responsible for the list – perhaps to make herself indispensable?
- But though the speaker contemplates an escape from the loft to the sky's wide open spaces and freedom, he still remains emotionally attached to his mother (through the metaphor of the measuring tape connecting them).
- We do not know if he has the power to let go, so the struggle for separation is by no means won.

'EDEN ROCK'

- The mother Causley creates in 'Eden Rock' is described with great warmth, even reverence, as 'Her hair, the colour of wheat, takes on the light' (8). The effect on the reader is to conjure up the image of a halo, particularly since there are other biblical connotations, (most obviously the Garden of Eden, or Paradise).
- The speaker's parents 'are waiting' (1) patiently for their child, now a grown man, possibly an elderly one. This is his conviction.
- It is as if the speaker has held the boyhood memory of Eden Rock close to him all his life. When the time comes to cross from life to death, one of the poem's main themes, he knows it will be relieved through his parents' patient love, another main theme.

KEY CONTEXT **A03**

Heaney has said that the craft of verse often appears in his poems unwittingly. He noted that in 'Follower' the turn of the plough at the end of the field has links to 'versus' in Latin, which means 'turn' or 'turn back'. 'Verse', meaning 'a line of poetry' and also 'turning to make another line', also comes from 'versus'. Poets often find things in their poems they had no intention of saying.

TOP TIP **A01**

Find images in 'Climbing My Grandfather' that show how the speaker becomes closer to his grandfather through the act of climbing him. For example, what effect does the image 'I …/place my feet/gently in the old stitches' (10–12) create for the reader? What themes do the images reinforce?

Love and desire

- 'Love's Philosophy': The speaker explores the nature of love.

- 'Sonnet 29 – "I think of thee!"': The speaker celebrates her profound love.

- 'Singh Song': A newly married bridegroom recounts his love for his unconventional wife.

THEME: LOVE AND DESIRE

In the cluster the theme of love and desire between men and women is expressed in different ways. Sometimes it is:

- playful and seductive, as in 'Love's Philosophy'
- renewed, as in the repairing of the relationship in 'Winter Swans'
- passionate, which is evident in Sonnet 29 – 'I think of thee'
- romantic, as in 'Singh Song!'.

In 'Letters From Yorkshire' it is not certain whether the love expressed is close friendship or more than that.

KEY QUOTATION: FINDING THE MAIN THEME (A01)

Three lines highlight the main theme in Shelley's 'Love's Philosophy': 'Nothing in the world is single;/All things by a law divine/in one another's being mingle' (5–7). Love shares the same philosophy as the natural world: one thing complements another. So humans, who also belong to the natural world, should follow the same philosophy and come together in love. However, you should also remember the speaker's purpose in presenting the argument: to seduce the other person.

EXAM FOCUS: WRITING ABOUT EFFECTS (A02)

Read what one student has written about how the poet presents the themes in 'Winter Swans'.

> In 'Winter Swans', Owen Sheers has used the metaphor of the swans to highlight the difference between the swans and the estranged couple, since the birds are 'in unison'. Through their example the couple are able to overcome their differences and become reconciled. However, the comment made by the partner that swans 'mate for life' also has an effect. It suggests that the couple intend to be together for life and that their differences were temporary. So we can say that another theme ...

Sound use of a literary term

Good choice of vocabulary to highlight the initial state of the couple's relationship

Good example of an effect that creates another theme in the poem

Now you try it:

Finish the sentence to say what you think the theme is.

'SONNET 29 – "I THINK OF THEE!"'

- Although passionate love is a theme in Elizabeth Barrett Browning's sonnet, its underlying tone suggests a love that is lasting.

- This underlying tone runs through the **quatrains** and the **sestet**, despite shifts in the tone of the argument typical of a **Petrarchan sonnet**.

- For example, in the lines 'be it understood/I will not have my thoughts instead of thee/Who art dearer, better!' (5–7) there is no suggestion of the writer being in love with the idea of love, or that her love is superficial.

- The poet's choice of adjectives such as, 'strong' (8) and 'deep' (12) suggest permanence, while 'a new air' (13) suggests transformation through a love that is special.

- Therefore, another theme in the poem could be 'true love'.

AIMING HIGH: LINKS BETWEEN THEMES

Show that you can see connections between various themes to give a fuller picture of a poem. For example, there are obvious connections between marriage, romance and desire in Daljit Negra's 'Singh Song!'. The speaker's 'newly bride' (5) is tapping her 'high heel' (18) in the flat above the shop. The married couple stare at the moon in the 'midnight hour' (43) and murmur romantic endearments. Both pursue their desires, sometimes together, sometimes not, when the new bride is drawn to her 'Sikh lover' (20) website. The theme of identity has less obvious links, but connections can still be made. It is most evident in the poet's presentation of the new bride and her idea of how she should lead her life. She is her own person, and we can assume uses her 'tiny eyes ov a gun' (28) to make her position clear. However, it is her 'effing' (23) at the speaker's mother (and also the speaker's defiance of his father) that marks out the new identity that this marriage will help shape. It is an identity that has little regard for the older generation and their values.

'LETTERS FROM YORKSHIRE'

- The poet is writing about a long distance relationship, but the nature of the relationship is unclear.

- Is the relationship a close friendship, or does it include a love relationship and therefore physical intimacy? The noun 'souls' (15) implies closeness.

- We are told 'It's not romance' (5), but 'romance' can refer to mystery as well as love. So the quotation could as easily apply to the beauty of the lapwings, evoked in verse one, as simply the wonder of nature, as to any comment on the relationship. Perhaps it applies to both.

THEME TRACKER A01

Breakdown and betrayal

- **(27–29)** The lover begins to question his hopeless situation.

- **(32–35)** His mood shifts. He believes Porphyria loves him and so he considers 'what to do' (35).

- **(36–60)** He strangles her, and sits with the body into the night, deluded in his certainty that he has done what Porphyria wanted.

THEME: BREAKDOWN AND BETRAYAL

- Several poems deal with the themes of breakdown and/or betrayal in love relationships.
- All express suffering and conflict and leave the reader with the sense that the collapse of the relationship is complete.
- 'The Farmer's Bride' portrays breakdown in a marriage.
- 'Neutral Tones' portrays breakdown in either a marriage or a long-term relationship; it is unclear which.
- 'When We Two Parted' includes both breakdown and betrayal.
- 'Porphyria's Lover', the most disturbing poem in the collection, depicts the end of a relationship as a result of the speaker's instability.

KEY QUOTATION: BETRAYAL A02

The sense of betrayal that the speaker feels in 'When We Two Parted' leads him to ask 'Why wert though so dear? (20). By asking a question, Byron creates a tone of puzzlement in the speaker's voice. The caesura both before and after the quotation creates a stop, as though the speaker had been halted in his tracks. Is he no longer under love's illusion? Is the loved one no longer worthy of his love? If so, he still 'grieve[s]' (26) for the relationship and is troubled by the deception she committed. Perhaps Byron is conveying the confusion of feelings that accompany the breakdown of an intimate relationship.

EXAM FOCUS: WRITING ABOUT EFFECTS A02

Read what one student has written about a theme of breakdown in 'Porphyria's Lover'.

> Shows how Browning creates effects

In 'Porphyria's Lover' Browning creates ambiguity by leaving the lover's reason for the murder of Porphyria unclear. The poet presents him as 'as one so pale/For love of' Porphyria. Is the lover physically ill, or lovesick, or both? The words that immediately follow, 'and all in vain', suggest that his love for her is a hopeless one. Is he jealous, perhaps, of Porphyria's life away from the cottage? There is no clear motive for the crime, and the overall effect Browning creates by using ambiguity is to highlight the theme of mental instability.

> Use of a rhetorical question enhances the style of writing

> Good choice of vocabulary to show reason for the crime

> More on how Browning creates effects

Now you try it:

Add a sentence to say how ambiguity affects how the reader regards the speaker.

REVISION FOCUS: TRACING DISCORD

Reread 'The Farmer's Bride'.

- Draw a timeline either vertically or horizontally on the page.
- Note all instances of the theme of discord or hostility between the wife and the farmer. Include important short quotations or line numbers.

The relationship between the farmer and his wife is broken from the beginning. However, do you think the estrangement between them grows worse? Study your notes and write a paragraph to explain.

TOP TIP: WRITING ABOUT SIMILARITIES AND DIFFERENCES A02

Remember, you can explore two poems (or more) to see if they share a theme by looking at the differences and similarities between them. For example betrayal in 'When We Two Parted' is foregrounded, so we can readily assume that the line 'Thy vows are all broken' (13) signifies betrayal. However, it would be difficult to apply the theme to 'Singh Song!'. The poem has a joyous tone, revealed in the intimacy between the bride and husband. Most of all, the husband's absence of jealousy despite his wife's activity on the 'Sikh lover' (20) website means that betrayal would be an inappropriate description. Another poem, 'Porphyria's Lover', poses a different question. Could we call the speaker's crime an act of betrayal as well as murder? If so, in what sense?

KEY CONTEXT A03

In Charlotte Mew's family there was mental instability, and Charlotte and her sister promised each other they would never marry in case their children were affected. There is some speculation that Charlotte Mew did not want to marry anyway, so the theme of 'The Farmer's Bride' could have autobiographical links. However, be careful not to overstate any such possibility.

THEME: SEPARATION

- All the poems, with the exception of one, deal with the theme of separation in some guise.

- It can be loose, as in 'Love's Philosophy', in which the efforts of the speaker focus on coming together rather than being apart.

- It can be extreme, as in 'Porphyria's Lover', in which the separation is irrevocable.

- Only in 'Singh Song!' is there no sense of separation in any of the relationships depicted (though there may be parental conflict). As a comic poem 'Singh Song!' is by its nature happy, which relates to its main themes of romantic love and desire.

AIMING HIGH: PARADOX

The contrast between the lives of the speaker and the letter-writer is an obvious feature of 'Letters from Yorkshire'. However, you can gain more marks if you look more closely at the links between **separation** and **connection** in the poem. Maura Dooley has evoked both these themes at the same time, which is a paradox. Since the speaker and the other person are apart, they are by definition separate. But they are in touch with each other through the postal service (and we assume email) so they are making connections. How does the poet emphasise this clever paradox? These contrary themes are highlighted in the poet's choice of words, through 'icy miles' (15) for example. While 'miles' reminds us of the distance between the speaker and the other person, 'icy' tells us the two share the same season; a winter in February. The paradox is particularly well expressed when *separately* 'in different houses' (14) they watch 'the same news' (14) *together*. Try to find other examples of this paradox.

THEME: TIME AND MEMORY

- The themes of time and memory are often linked to separation.

- In 'Neutral Tones', 'Walking Away', 'Eden Rock' and 'Winter Swans' the memory of a particular time and place is the focus of the poems, which also feature separation between two or more people.

- Memory in the form of the son's recollections of childhood is an important theme in the relationship between father and son in 'Follower'.

- Time features in 'When We Two Parted', and takes us from the poem's past to the poem's present and into the imagined future of two people who are separated.

- Time and distance are central to the love and friendship in 'Letters from Yorkshire' in their communications with each other.

- The farmer's failed marriage in 'The Farmer's Bride' covers three years.

- 'Before You Were Mine' and 'Climbing My Grandfather' take leaps into the past; the former as an imagined experience, the latter to resurrect a memory of a grandparent. In both, the speakers are separated from the loved one.

TOP TIP: WRITING ABOUT MEMORY (A01)

Notice how in 'Neutral Tones' Hardy threads the theme of memory throughout almost the entire poem. In verse one the speaker describes the 'white' (2) sun, remembers the tree was an 'ash' (4), recalls how 'few leaves' (3) there were and how the 'sod' (earth) was 'starving' (3). The detail increases in verse two and three to recall the expression in the eyes and mouth of the other person. We know too that the memory is long-standing from references to the past, such as 'years ago' (6) and 'Since then' (13). The effect Hardy creates is to drive home to the reader just how much a potent memory endures.

THEME: THE NATURAL WORLD

- Nature is evoked in many different ways in the collection.
- Sometimes it is the rural setting of the poem, for example in 'The Farmer's Bride' or 'Winter Swans'.
- Or it is used to describe passionate thoughts and feelings, as in 'Sonnet 29 – "I think of thee!"'.
- Sometimes, as in 'Love's Philosophy', it is a device to present an argument.
- At other times it is a metaphor for a person, as the mountain is for the grandparent in Andrew Waterhouse's 'Climbing My Grandfather'.
- It is a sinister force in 'Porphyria's Lover', but a benign one in 'Eden Rock'.

THEME TRACKER (A01)

The Natural World

- 'Love's Philosophy: The poet compares human love with nature.

- 'Neutral Tones': The speaker compares his dead relationship with winter.

- 'Letters from Yorkshire': The speaker imagines her friend's country life as 'seeing the seasons' (6).

KEY QUOTATION: THE WINGED SEED (A01)

Cecil Day Lewis conjures up a particularly powerful simile of the natural world in 'Walking Away', when he describes the movements of his young son as he leaves him: 'eddying away/Like a winged seed loosened from its parent stem' (11, 12). A sycamore seed has small delicate wings, and is almost certainly the 'winged seed' in the poem. When sycamore seeds cast off from the plant they spin in the breeze in what appears to be a haphazard fashion, as does the child in the poem. As he casts off from his 'parent stem' (his father) he is literally unable to find a straight route alone. This conveys his vulnerability.

REVISION FOCUS: NATURE

Reread 'Eden Rock'.

Draw a spider diagram in the following way:

- Write 'The Natural World' in the centre of a piece of paper. Add arrows around it that lead to five boxes, one for each verse.
- Find all the images and vocabulary that evoke the natural world, and the seasons and weather.
- Then search for those that may not describe the natural world directly, but reinforce the idea of it – for example 'sprigged dress' (5).
- Record your findings in the correct boxes.
- Write a short paragraph saying how Causley uses the natural world to create effects.

CONTEXTS

THE ROMANTICS

Romanticism originated in the late eighteenth century and flourished during the early to mid nineteenth century in the arts, particularly in poetry. The movement arose partly as a reaction to the effects of the Industrial Revolution and the existing attitudes that favoured logic and reason above feeling, and in which the individual experience was lost.

AIMING HIGH: IN LOVE WITH LOVE?

To develop your ideas you should look more closely at the nature of feeling conveyed by the Romantics. 'Intensity' is the key word. By placing emphasis on emotion rather than reason, they are highlighting the belief that true poetry should be created through feeling. This quality is especially marked in Byron's 'When We Two Parted', and the poem is frequently discussed as though it reflects real life. Though there may be an autobiographical element, it can be overstated. Through its emphasis on intensity, the poem embodies the values of the Romantic poets. Byron may have drawn on a range of personal experiences, or on none. You could consider presenting an argument that suggests the poet is exploring an idea – the nature and 'Sorrow' (8) of love betrayed.

THE GOTHIC

- The strong feelings expressed by the Romantic poets might include such emotions as wonder, grief or distress. In the Gothic, which has close links to Romanticism, it would become horror.
- The typical Gothic narrative has common settings: rugged landscapes, ruins, secret places, isolation and extreme weather, all of which might be sinister.
- The storyline involves mystery, the supernatural, crime or transgression.
- Characters often follow their desires and may experience nightmares and insanity. This in turn has links to an interest in the workings of the mind, the psyche, which would eventually become what we call psychology.
- Browning's 'Porphyria's Lover' has links to the early Victorian Gothic and shows an interest in the psyche.

KEY CONTEXT: THE POSITION OF VICTORIAN WOMEN

In Charlotte Mew's 'The Farmer's Bride', the farmer's expectations of his bride are misplaced. He assumes, that though 'Too young maybe' (2) she would conform to the pattern of a dutiful wife. But fear prevents intimacy. She remains 'her wild self' (33) – untamed rather than controlled. The poem indirectly questions the Victorian assumption that women should be constrained.

TOP TIP A01

Although they are very different in tone, try to find at least one similarity between 'When We Two Parted' by Byron and Shelley's 'Love's Philosophy'. For example, consider the nature of the feeling expressed in the quotations: 'Sunk chill on my brow' (10) from 'When We Two Parted' and 'See the mountains kiss high Heaven' (9) from 'Love's Philosophy'.

KEY CONTEXT A03

Notice the hints in 'Porphyria's Lover' that the two come from different social backgrounds. He lives in an isolated cottage, suggesting low status. Porphyria wears a cloak, a shawl and gloves, suggesting that she is not poor. Consider how different backgrounds might have a bearing on the relationship.

AIMING HIGH: THE VICTORIAN IDEAL

It is important to explore social relationships if the task allows it. In contrast to Porphyria and the farmer's bride, a woman who does conform to the Victorian ideal is the speaker in Elizabeth Barrett Browning's 'Sonnet 29 – "I think of thee!"'. She is like the clinging vine, under the protection of the man, the 'strong tree' (8). It is 'within' his 'shadow' (13) that the female speaker finds her place. In the Victorian period, this picture satisfied the popular view of how and what a female poet should write. The voice should focus on love as opposed to themes regarded as suitable for men, such as justice or war. The voice should also be yielding, as it is in the sonnet, which comes from *Sonnets from the Portuguese*. Consequently in the popular imagination (though not necessarily in Victorian literary circles) the sonnets overshadowed Elizabeth Barrett Browning's other work, such as *Aurora Leigh*, a novel in verse. That work is an attempt to challenge the conventional view of womanhood. You may wish to explore this other voice that the poet creates and consider in what ways it contrasts with the voice in 'Sonnet 29 – "I think of thee!"'.

TOP TIP (A03)

Remember self-mockery is a kind of **irony**, used for comic effect, as in the title 'Singh Song!'. It is used to attack negative stereotypes that result from different kinds of prejudice, by taking possession of the insult and mocking it.

CULTURAL CONTEXTS

'Before You Were Mine'

Carol Ann Duffy presents a Scottish setting in 'Before You Were Mine', with its references to Glasgow's 'George Square' (13) and Edinburgh's 'Portobello' (18) district. There is also a distinctly Scottish/Irish/Gaelic tone with the surnames 'McGeeney' and 'Duff'. The **idioms** 'pals' (2) and 'hiding' (10) (punishment) and 'Ma' (9) also suggest a Northern/Gaelic vernacular.

'Singh Song!'

Daljit Nagra's poetry plays with the language of English speakers whose first language is Punjabi, and he draws on both British and Indian cultures. He also challenges stereotypical views of British Asians.

EXAM FOCUS: WRITING ABOUT CONTEXT (A03)

Read what one student has written about the stereotype Daljit Nagra challenges.

> *A clear opening with an appropriate use of a technical term*

The title of the poem 'Singh Song!' is a pun, because 'Singh' has a double meaning. It is the surname adopted by all Sikh men and is a Punjabi word meaning 'lion'. So at one level we could say that the poem is a song by a British Sikh for his bride. However, 'sing-song' also refers to a voice that repeatedly rises and falls. So the poet may also have chosen the title to draw attention to the negative stereotype of the 'sing-song' voice that has been attributed to British Asian speakers by those with prejudiced viewpoints.

> *A necessary connective to qualify an important point*

> *Well-presented analysis of the effects intended by the poet*

Now you try it:

Complete the sentence to show what the quotation implies about the speaker.

PROGRESS AND REVISION CHECK

SECTION ONE: CHECK YOUR KNOWLEDGE

Answer these quick questions to test your basic knowledge of the themes and contexts of the poems.

1 In which of these poems is the main theme family ties: 'Porphyria's Lover', 'When We Two Parted' or 'Eden Rock'?

2 Which poems come from the Romantic period?

3 In which poem is one of the main themes communication?

4 What poem has links to the Gothic?

5 In 'Mother, any distance', what theme does the reel of tape signify?

6 In which poem is 'letting go' a theme?

7 In which poem is love compared to a 'deep joy'?

8 Which poems explore multicultural contexts?

9 In what period was 'Sonnet 29 – "I think of thee!"' written?

10 Name five kinds of love that appear in the cluster.

SECTION TWO: CHECK YOUR UNDERSTANDING

Here is a task about a theme in a poem. This requires more thought and a longer response. Try to write at least three to four paragraphs.

Task: How does verse three of 'The Farmer's Bride' reveal attitudes to women at the time the poem was written? Think about:

- What happens to the wife in the poem
- The speaker's attitude

PROGRESS CHECK

GOOD PROGRESS

I can:

- Explain the main themes and contexts of the poems and how they contribute to the effect on the reader. ☐
- Use a range of appropriate evidence to support any points I make about these elements. ☐

EXCELLENT PROGRESS

I can:

- Analyse in detail the way themes are developed and presented across the poems. ☐
- Refer closely to key aspects of context and the implications they have for the poets' viewpoints, and the interpretation of relationships and ideas. ☐

FORM

What is form?	The way the poem is laid out on the page, or a specific set of rules or typical features a poem follows, such as those for a sonnet, or a lyric poem. A poem's shape or form can often enhance meaning.
Example	'Love's Philosophy' is a lyric poem of the Romantic period. Typically it has repeated stanza lengths, regular line lengths and patterns, and a regular metre.
Effect	The effect of the repeating patterns is to reinforce the expression of intense personal emotion in the poem.

KEY CONTEXT (A03)

Traditionally, an important feature of a good poem was how well it followed the rules of a particular form. Today, poetic forms are more flexible. It is left to the individual poet to decide how they want to present their poem.

- Each poem in the cluster has its own shape or form, which helps to express the ideas and feelings the poet wants to communicate.
- Some poems follow traditional models while others, usually the modern poems, create their own.
- Examples of traditional models are the dramatic monologue of 'Porphyria's Lover', and the sonnet of 'Sonnet 29 – "I think of thee!"'.
- Other organising devices that affect the shape of the poem might be repeated stanzas, quatrains, octaves (such as 'When We Two Parted') and tercets (such as 'Letters from Yorkshire') found in poems from the past and the present.
- The modern poems are often free verse and create their own shapes or modify existing forms.
- However, even free verse usually has some organising feature, such as repetition. For example, the use of the chorus in 'Singh Song!'.

TOP TIP: THE SONNET FORM (A01)

The Petrarchan sonnet has a specific form. It has fourteen lines in which both quatrains have the rhyme scheme *abba*. The sestet that follows can vary. For the sestet 'Sonnet 29 – "I think of thee!"' Elizabeth Barrett Browning has chosen the scheme *cbcbcb.* In the first quatrain we are presented with the speaker's reflections 'as thoughts' that 'twine' (1) about her lover. He is ever present in her mind, until she is so overwhelmed with thoughts of him that 'there's nought to see' (3). By the second quatrain these thoughts are now in conflict with the speaker's desire to have her lover with her. The sestet marks a shift in tone, the 'turn' or volta signalled by the change in the rhyme scheme. This shift is the final comment on the situation, which in this case brings about a suggested resolution. What is this resolution?

CHECKPOINT 15 (A02)

What change of font is used in 'Singh Song!'? Why do you think this is?

EXAM FOCUS: WRITING ABOUT EFFECTS (A02)

Read what one student has written about how 'Eden Rock' is set out, and the effects created.

> **A sound example of a verse form**

Charles Causley's poem 'Eden Rock' is written in quatrains for the first four verses. The effect of the quatrains, along with the line lengths, which are similar from verse to verse (except for the first and last lines of the poem) create an easy shape and movement. So as the speaker recounts the childhood memory to the reader we have a sense of regularity (helped along by the repeating full rhyme and half-rhyme (such as 'dress'/'grass'). This repetition seems to reinforce the images of the picnic scene 'beyond Eden Rock' as a well-known memory, as though the speaker has thought of it often. In the final verse the shape changes and the last line (which is also in a different tense) is set apart.

> **Shows the effect on the audience**

> **Shows how Causley creates effects**

Now you try it:

Add a sentence to explain the effects of the way the last line of the poem is set apart.

FORM AND CHANGE

- You need to be alert to the way different poems are set out, and what effects are created.
- Notice changes in repeating forms (as in 'Eden Rock', and many modern poems).
- Change usually exists to draw attention to particular feelings expressed.

AIMING HIGH: DRAMATIC MONOLOGUE ⭐

This particular form allows the poet to present a narrative through a persona. So in 'Porphyria's Lover' Robert Browning chooses the single voice of the murderer to address us. We follow the speaker's calculating yet intimate actions, which are also disturbingly precise in their detail, 'and all her hair/In one long yellow string' (38, 39) he winds 'Three times her little throat around' (40). The effect on the reader is chilling. Explore the nature of the dramatic monologue further to gain more marks. In what way is it like theatre, as well as narrative? What is the relationship with the speaker/persona and the reader? What aspect of the story, characters or setting makes us curious?

> **CHECKPOINT 16** (A02)
>
> In 'The Farmer's Bride' there is a change in the length of the fourth verse. What name would you give the verse? What effect does it help to create?

STRUCTURE

What is structure?	Poems have underlying patterns and structures that can reveal their development and changes.
Example	In 'Love's Philosophy', the speaker presents an argument to a potential lover. He suggests that pairings in nature are the natural order of things, and therefore natural for humans too. He concludes the argument by asking what are these pairings in nature worth if he and the lover do not come together.
Effect	The effect of the argument is to further the speaker's desires and win the potential lover.

- The structure of a poem is the underlying pattern that reveals its development.

- There is a wide range of structures in the cluster, and some poems combine patterns. For example, in 'When We Two Parted' there are shifts through time from the past in verse one, to past and present in verse two, present in verse three and a combination of past, present and future in the final verse. The importance given to past, present and future in turn gives weight to the intense feelings expressed.

- Other poems seem to have a structure that we can recognise from the outset. A mountain helps to structure the poem 'Climbing My Grandfather'. But the journey the mountaineer/speaker takes is just as important, if not more so, because it conveys his changing emotions.

- The structure of 'Neutral Tones' is less clear, but by the time the reader has reached the final verse they realise that the speaker has explored the feelings sufficiently to condense them into the words 'love deceives' (13).

REVISION FOCUS: TRACKING THE STRUCTURE

Reread 'Climbing My Grandfather'. Be aware of the stages the grandson makes in his journey.

- Draw a vertical timeline.

- Note the stages of the climb, beginning at the bottom of the timeline. For example, when he begins the climb, he decides 'to do it free, without a rope or net./First the old brogues' (1, 2). You could note 'no rope or net, begins with the shoes'.

- End at the top of the timeline when the grandson reaches the summit.

Why do you think the grandson made the climb? What changes has he undergone? Consider what the climb reveals about the grandson's relationship with his grandfather. Write a paragraph about how the structure of the poem shows the poem's development.

TOP TIP **A02**

Notice how some poems combine form and structure. 'Sonnet 29 – "I think of thee!"' has a specific form (two quatrains, the sestet and the couplet) and also shows the change and development of the speaker's feelings from initial reflections, through conflict, turn and resolution. The form and pattern would have evolved over a long period of time to become the Petrarchan sonnet.

EXAM FOCUS: WRITING ABOUT EFFECTS · A02

Read what one student has written about the structure of 'Walking Away'.

> **Sound opening sentence and good use of a literary technique**

In 'Walking Away' the structure of the poem begins as the speaker describes the past memory as a scene in the first three verses. The meaning of the memory is something the speaker can 'never quite grasp to convey'. The poem develops as he reflects on his feelings so that by the last verse he is able to convey the meaning of the memory. The reader learns two things. The first, 'selfhood begins with a walking away' (19) is true for all children growing up, who must strike out on their own. The second ...

> **Shows how the structure progresses and how a difficulty is resolved**

> **Shows the effect on the reader**

Now you try it:

Finish the sentence to explain that what the poem is saying is true for all parents.

REVISION FOCUS: FROM BEGINNING TO END

Reread 'Winter Swans'.

- Draw four large boxes, one above the other, in which to write.
- Label them in order, top down: 'Verses 1, 2', 'Verses 3, 4', 'Verses 5, 6', 'Couplet'.
- Write notes in each box to identify how the poem is structured. In particular, as you read through the poem, note how the poem progresses from beginning to end, any changes that occur, and if there any resolutions.
- When you have completed your notes, use them to write a paragraph about the structure of the poem.

TOP TIP · A02

Whenever you study the structure of a poem, always search for a turning point or points. If there is more than one, try to decide which is the most important, and why. Remember that a turning point does not necessarily mean a happy resolution to a problem or conflict.

RHYME, RHYTHM AND SOUND

- The rhythm of a poem usually reflects its meaning. If the rhythm is quickened or slowed this will be to create an effect. Compare the increase in rhythm in the last verse of 'The Farmer's Wife', as the farmer's desire increases, with the slow final line of 'Eden Rock', where the speaker confronts his own mortality.

- **Metre** is a traditional way of organising rhythm into a strict pattern. In free verse, the rhythm may follow a given pattern, but less strictly and it usually varies within the poem. Free verse also tends to follow the cadence of speech.

What is metre?	It is the pattern of stressed and unstressed syllables in a line of verse. **Iambic pentameter** is the most common metre in English poetry.
Example	'Sonnet 29 – "I think of thee!"' is written in iambic pentameter. The line starts with an unstressed syllable followed by a stressed syllable for five iambic feet (a foot is the varied stress in a unit of rhythm): 'Put **out** broad **leaves** and **soon** there's **nought** to **see**' (3).
Effect	Iambic pentameter suits the rhythms of English because it sounds natural. It is the traditional metre of the **Petrarchan sonnet**.

- Rhyme works closely with rhythm and helps to move the poem along. Often, the more perfect the rhyme and **rhyme scheme**, the more accented the rhythm. For example, 'Love's Philosophy' has full **end rhyme**, and the repeated rhyme scheme is *ababcdcd*.

- Most of the traditional poems in the cluster have full end rhyme and metre. **Free verse** may appear to be without rhyme, but rhyme is usually present, if less obviously. For example, 'earth' (4) and 'breath' (5) in 'Winter Swans' draw attention to the drenched earth (it is **personified**) as though it were struggling not to drown.

TOP TIP: WRITING ABOUT RHYTHM (A01)

Notice that sometimes the rhythm is the opposite of what we might expect. In 'Porphyria's Lover', Browning chooses to retain the steady metre (**iambic tetrameter**) before and during the murder. 'I found/A thing to do' (37, 38) says the speaker, prepares the murder, and adds 'And strangled her' (41). The blunt statement remains part of the established rhythm of the poem because the murder is one carried out by an unstable character who does not grasp the difference between right and wrong. The **caesura** in the middle of line 41 has limited effect on the rhythm. Rather, it adds to the cruelty of the act.

TOP TIP (A02)

Remember that full rhyme can occur within a line, not only at the end of a poem. For example 'light' (13) and 'night' (14) are **internal rhymes** in 'Letters from Yorkshire'. The effect is to create a subtle, mysterious and even romantic mood, reflecting the sense of communication between 'other world[s]' (12).

TOP TIP (A02)

Notice the **cadence** of a line or stanza, and ask yourself if it is creating any particular effect that is important to the poem. Sometimes cadence can be very marked, as in the line 'Hey Singh, ver yoo bin?' (12) from 'Singh Song!'. The rise and fall can be easily felt in the line, which is part of a chorus. The chorus, in turn, is like a song and suits the title and style of the poem. The cadence also heightens the humour of the chorus.

CAESURA

What is caesura?	A pause during a line of poetry that affects the pace and rhythm.
Example	'The brown of her – her eyes, her hair, her hair!' (46) from 'The Farmer's Bride'.
Effect	The effect of the caesura is to bring the words and pace to a sudden halt, almost like a gasp. It stresses the desire the farmer feels for his wife, while for the reader it strikes a sinister note.

ENJAMBMENT

What is enjambment?	When a line runs on into the next without pause, carrying the thought, pace and sometimes the sound with it. Also called run-on lines.
Example	'The winds of Heaven mix for ever / With a sweet emotion' (3, 4) from 'Love's Philosophy'.
Effect	The first line flows into the second, taking the light rhythmic movement of the poem with it, and also emphasises the mix of winds and emotion, so reinforcing the idea of togetherness in the poem.

ALLITERATION

What is alliteration?	When the same sound is repeated in a stretch of language, usually at the beginning of words.
Example	'righting in rough weather' (12) from 'Winter Swans'.
Effect	The effect of the 'r' sound rolling on the tongue (particularly if we read the words aloud) reinforces the image of the swans 'like boats' (12) as they bob up again from the water.

TOP TIP (A01)

Note that in 'Eden Rock' half-rhyme occurs throughout the poem, with only occasional full rhyme. (For example, 'Rock'/'Jack' (1, 3) and 'suit'/'feet' (2, 4) in the first verse are half-rhymes.) The effect is to make the language sound easy and natural. What undesired effect might have occurred if the poet had used full rhyme entirely?

ASSONANCE

What is assonance?	When the same vowel sound is repeated in the same place in a stretch of language.
Example	'where you sparkle and waltz and laugh' (20) from 'Before You were Mine'.
Effect	The repetition of the long 'a' sound suggests the exclamation 'Ah!', implying wonder. In effect the 'a' sound heightens the sense of glamour that the speaker describes.

LANGUAGE

VOICE AND VIEWPOINT

What is voice?	The way the speaker of the poem is created in the reader's mind.
Example	The farmer in 'The Farmer's Bride' has a distinctive voice. For example he says, ''twasn't' (7), which is a shortened version of 'it wasn't'. He also uses a non-standard version of the verb 'to be', as in 'her be' (10) instead of using the standard English 'she is'.
Effect	The effect is to create a rural **dialect**, which in turn convinces the reader that the narrative is authentic and reliable.

There are many different kinds of voices in the cluster, but most poems are addressed through the voice of an unnamed speaker.

- Occasionally the speaker is given a specific identity, a persona that the poet has decided to use. For example, the farmer in 'The Farmer's Bride', which is a narrative poem.
- The perspective from which the poem is expressed is the point of view. It is usually expressed in either first person 'I' or third person 'he' or 'she'.
- Quite often the second-person point of view is included with the first. 'When We Two Parted' has a first-person speaker who addresses an ex-lover as 'Thy' (13) or 'thee' (17) (second person, 'you').

AIMING HIGH: A SHIFTING VOICE ⭐

In 'Letters from Yorkshire' there are subtle changes in the voice. At first the reader may not notice these, because the poet has effortlessly changed who is being addressed. For example in verse one the speaker seems to be talking to the reader, commenting on her friend's reported observations in the third person, when 'he saw the first lapwings' (2) in the garden. In verse two the perspective shifts. The speaker addresses the friend in the second person. Is she calling to him over the miles, 'You out there, in the cold' (6)? Or is the speaker addressing her friend in her mind? Either way, the effect is to give a greater sense of immediacy and closeness to the relationship. In verse three the speaker asks a **rhetorical question** in line nine, expects no answer from the letter-writer, but provides one in verse four, again as though she is contemplating. Explore the effects of the voice in the final verse. Think about the use of the personal pronoun 'our' (15).

TOP TIP (A02)

Remember that the voice the reader hears is not the voice of the poet. That is why the term 'speaker' is used. Poems are rarely truly autobiographical, if at all. They are always works of the imagination. Any experience the poet uses is recreated.

CHECKPOINT 17 (A02)

What is the voice like in 'Walking Away'? What is the speaker's viewpoint? Who are they speaking to?

IMAGERY

- **Imagery** makes ideas vivid through an appeal to the senses, most frequently sight.
- It includes common techniques such as **simile** and **metaphor**.
- Characters are created through imagery. There are, in particular, two contrasting images of children. Heaney creates a boisterous, cheerful image of the speaker as a boy riding on his father's back. In 'Walking Away' a simile describes the son like 'a winged seed loosened from the parent stem' (12), so that the boy seems lost.
- Nature imagery is very common in the cluster and often conjures up place and setting, such as the rural landscape in 'The Farmer's Bride', or in 'Winter Swans'.
- The lushest use of nature imagery is the depiction of the 'wild vines' (2), 'broad leaves' (3) and 'straggling green' (4) that typify the speaker's thoughts in 'Sonnet 29 – "I think of thee!"'.

KEY QUOTATION: AUTUMN (A01)

'The short days shorten and the oaks are brown,/The blue smoke rises to the low grey sky' (34, 35) are spoken by the farmer in 'The Farmer's Bride'. Autumn has arrived and the year is declining. The colours 'brown' and 'grey' are melancholy ones, reflecting the farmer's emotions. 'The short days shorten' (34) suggests that the days are drifting away like the vanishing 'blue smoke' (35). This image of the fading year is reinforced by the soft, **alliterative** 'sh' that appeals to the sense of sound. But the most important effect created is the idea that time is running out for any good to come of the farmer's marriage. You could compare the images from the natural world in 'The Farmer's Bride' with those in 'Neutral Tones'. Are their effects similar or not?

TOP TIP (A02)

A **motif** is a recurring idea, object, theme (or other figure). In 'The Farmer's Bride' an animal motif continually occurs and is linked to the young bride, who is untamed, voiceless and innocent, like the animals she loves.

METAPHOR

What is metaphor?	When one thing is used to describe another (usually dissimilar), creating a striking image. An extended metaphor continues the image or an aspect of it, sometimes throughout the poem.
Example	'the line still feeding out' (7), 'Anchor. Kite' (8), 'I space-walk' (9) from 'Mother, any distance'.
Effect	The 'line' (7) is a measuring tape connecting mother to son, and represents their relationship. The metaphor of the measuring tape is an **extended metaphor** because it appears as the string of a kite and an astronaut tethered by a line to the spacecraft.

SYMBOLISM

What is symbolism?	When one thing represents another, usually with a meaning that is widely understood in a culture.
Example	'Eden Rock'.
Effect	The poet's choice of 'Eden' as a title cannot be by chance; it is a powerful and well-known religious symbol that in Christianity, for example, refers to the Garden of Eden, or Paradise. Eden Rock can therefore be understood as Paradise.

CONNOTATION

What is connotation?	An extra meaning or association we attach to a word or image in a specific situation (i.e. what it suggests to us).
Example	'ash' [tree] (4) from 'Neutral Tones'.
Effect	The type of tree, 'ash' (4), reminds us of the remnants of a fire, which suggests that the passion of the relationship has gone. 'ash' also reminds us of death, and the death of the relationship.

KEY CONTEXT (A02)

It is important to remember that connotations occur in specific contexts. For example an ash tree ('Neutral Tones') occurs in John Clare's 'Emmonsail's Heath in Winter'. Here the ash is part of a sad winter landscape, but one that is well loved by the speaker.

EXAM FOCUS: WRITING ABOUT EFFECTS (A02)

Read what one student has written about how verbs are used in 'Follower'.

A good opening sentence that illustrates a technique and its effects

Seamus Heaney presents a striking physical image of the speaker as a young boy, through using strong verbs, such as 'stumbled' and 'tripping', that seem to the reader to capture the clumsiness of a young child. These verbs are tied to other vivid images, such as 'hob-nailed wake', suggesting the footprint of sturdy farm boots on ploughed land. This means they have the effect of enhancing the comic picture of the determined child struggling, but not crying. Instead, he seemed to enjoy 'Yapping'.

Connective linking cause and effect

Quotation neatly embedded in the sentence

Now you try it:

Add a sentence to explain the effects of the verb 'Yapping' (22) and the way the reader sees the child.

LANGUAGE AND VOCABULARY CHOICE

- The style and language used in the cluster vary hugely.
- Some poets use what we now regard as **archaic** language. Vocabulary such as 'thine' (8) meaning 'yours' in 'Love's Philosophy', or 'nought' (3) meaning 'nothing' in 'Sonnet 29 – "I think of thee!"' are common to the period in which the poems were written.
- Certain modern poets use **colloquial** language. Everyday expressions such as 'You reckon it's worth it' (10) help to create the authentic picture of the mother as a teenager in Carol Ann Duffy's 'Before You Were Mine'.
- All poems use figurative language in some fashion. In 'Walking Away' the son is 'set free/Into a wilderness' (8, 9) as his father sees him leave in what the quotation suggests is bewilderment.

IRONY

What is irony?	Language used to say one thing but mean or suggest another, hidden, meaning.
Example	In 'Porphyria's Lover' the speaker says early in the poem as Porphyria arrives, 'She shut the cold out and the storm' (7).
Effect	At this stage the reader assumes that the lovers will have a tender encounter, safe from the violent storm outside. But we later learn that the violence is within the cottage, culminating in murder. Rather than shutting out the cold, Porphyria will become deathly cold.

OXYMORON

What is an oxymoron?	Language that juxtaposes meanings that seem to be contradictory.
Example	In 'Climbing My Grandfather' the speaker notes how the grandfather's finger feels like 'warm ice' (10).
Effect	The effect of the oxymoron is to make the grandfather's finger seem cold and warm at the same time: 'ice' evokes the ice on a mountain and implies that the grandfather is dead; 'warm' suggests the emotional warmth the speaker feels for his grandfather.

RHETORICAL QUESTION

What is a rhetorical question?	A question that expects no answer. It is asked in order to create an effect.
Example	At the end of 'When We Two Parted', the speaker asks 'How should I greet thee?' (31).
Effect	The intense sense of loss is heightened. Asking a question rather than making a statement at the end of the poem confronts the reader and has greater impact.

Questions in poetry are often rhetorical. If the speaker is addressing someone, the person cannot reply because they are not usually present in the poem. Exceptions occur when the poem includes dialogue or reported speech (as in 'Singh Song!'). As a rule, the poet will be using a question to create an effect of some kind. Remind yourself of the effect created by the rhetorical question at the end of 'Love's Philosophy'.

PERSONIFICATION

What is personification?	When ideas or things are given human feelings and characteristics.
Example	In 'Love's Philosophy' Nature is given human attributes throughout the poem, as in 'See the mountains kiss high Heaven' (9).
Effect	Giving human attributes to Nature furthers the speaker's argument that the potential lover should kiss him. If Nature is like humans and unites, this is all the more reason why a couple should unite with each other.

TOP TIP: WRITING ABOUT PERSONIFICATION (A02)

Apart from personifying Nature in 'Love's Philosophy', the poet also **personifies** the title and gives love the ability to think. The technique is used heavily in the poem, which is the main example of personification in the cluster, though several of the poems also personify Nature. In 'Porphyria's Lover' the wind is 'sullen' (2) and aggressive enough to 'vex the lake' (4). In hindsight we can see how malign nature mirrors the inner nature of the speaker, which is a destructive force. In 'Neutral Tones' the colourless leaves signal that nature is all but dead, reflecting the death of the relationship.

TONE AND MOOD

What is mood?	Mood or tone is the atmosphere created by an artistic work, such as a poem. It affects our feelings.
Example	'Rather, instantly/Renew thy presence' (7, 8) in 'Sonnet 29 – "I think of thee!"'.
Effect	The mood of urgency has been building from line 5, culminating in the adverb 'instantly' (7) and the imperative 'Renew' (8). The run-on line also helps to carry the mood along.

- Almost any feature in a poem can convey mood. Usually it is through image and sounds or rhythm and rhyme, but it can also be enhanced through punctuation, enjambment, caesura or any other technique.

- As the speaker climbs to the top of the house in 'Mother, any distance' still attached to the measuring tape and his mother, there is a mood of weariness in verse two. The enjambment, such as 'recording/length' (5, 6) and 'unreeling/years' (7, 8), as well as the lines that zigzag like the tape, enhances the mood.

- Some poems in the cluster have easily identifiable moods. The lightness and flow of 'Love's Philosophy' (evoked for example in the images of water) creates a sense of joy that is clear from the outset.

- Eden Rock seems luminous. Its brightness is partly created by the 'three' mysterious 'suns' (13), so that mystery is also an aspect of its mood.

REVISION FOCUS: DEFINING THE MOOD

Reread 'Singh Song!'. Try to sum up the general mood of the poem, and write down a few adjectives to describe it.

- Now look more closely at the poem. Draw a spider diagram for each verse. In the centre of each diagram write the verse number and 'Mood'.

- Look for subtle differences as the poem progresses. For example, in what way does the mood shift in verse three compared to verses one and two? Refer back to your original list of adjectives for comparison.

- Select quotations or note rhythms and rhyme (or any other techniques) in each verse that seem to highlight the mood. Record them on the spider diagrams.

When you have completed the diagrams, refer to your notes to write some paragraphs on the changing moods within the poem.

PROGRESS AND REVISION CHECK

SECTION ONE: CHECK YOUR KNOWLEDGE

Answer these quick questions to test your basic knowledge of the themes and contexts of the poems.

1. What extended metaphor is used in 'Climbing My Grandfather'?
2. Who speaks in a rural dialect, and in which poem?
3. The Petrarchan sonnet has two quatrains (or an octave) and what other verse form?
4. In which poem does the following image occur: 'globed like a full sail strung' – and what does it refer to?
5. In what metre is 'Sonnet 29 – "I think of thee!"' written?
6. What does a caesura do?
7. Where is the sibilant in the following: 'we skirted the lake, silent and apart' – and where does the quotation come from?
8. Where does internal rhyme occur?
9. What is cadence?
10. In which poem does the image of the 'God-curst' sun appear, and what does it represent?

SECTION TWO: CHECK YOUR UNDERSTANDING

Here is a task about the imagery the poet uses. This requires more thought and a longer response. Try to write at least three to four paragraphs.

Task: How does Owen Sheers show that love can be renewed in 'Winter Swans'? Think about:

- What poetic technique the poet uses
- What effects are created through the technique

PROGRESS CHECK

GOOD PROGRESS

I can:

- Explain how the poets use key poetic techniques to shape the poem, show relationships and develop ideas. ☐
- Use relevant quotations to support the points I make, and make reference to the effect of some techniques. ☐

EXCELLENT PROGRESS

I can:

- Analyse in detail the poets' use of particular techniques to convey ideas, create a voice or viewpoint and evoke mood or setting. ☐
- Select from a range of evidence, including apt quotations, to infer the effect of particular techniques and to develop wider interpretations. ☐

THE EXAM

In **Section B** of the exam you will be given one poem (printed on the exam paper) from the *Love and Relationships* cluster and asked to compare it with another poem from the cluster, of your own choice.

So, what sorts of things might you be asked to compare/contrast between poems? Here are three possibilities:

- Attitudes towards women
- Feelings expressed about family ties
- Themes that present different ideas about love

HOW WOULD THIS WORK FOR A GIVEN POEM?

A typical question might be:

Question: Compare how poets present ideas about how love is celebrated in 'Singh Song!' and one other poem from the collection you have studied.

WHAT POSSIBLE POEMS COULD 'SINGH SONG!' BE COMPARED WITH?

The examiners are looking for you to be able to draw links with any poem in the cluster – not just to revise a particular few – and that will be part of the skill you demonstrate, but clearly there are certain poems that are more closely linked in content than others. For example, in this case:

Like 'Singh Song!':

- 'Love's Philosophy' celebrates romantic love
- 'Letters from Yorkshire' celebrates affection
- 'Winter Swans' celebrates commitment in love.

HOW WOULD THIS RELATE TO AO1, 2 AND 3?

In 'Love's Philosophy', for example, the writer:

AO1
- presents pairings in nature, so that 'sunlight clasps the earth' (13) for example, suggests that love is a law of the natural world
- uses the pairings in nature as an argument to suggest that humans should also be in couples.

AO2
- uses nature imagery to create an ideal world in which 'one another's being' should 'mingle' (7) and create harmony
- moves the rhythm along easily to match the images of nature that flow into each other, as in, 'The fountains mingle with the river/And the rivers with the Ocean' (1, 2).

AO3
- In contrast to 'Singh Song!', which is a contemporary poem, 'Love's Philosophy' is a lyric poem from the Romantic movement
- 'Singh Song!' has an urban setting, while 'Love's Philosophy' has nature as a backdrop.

TOP TIP (A02)

Whenever you discuss rhyme, rhythm or metre you should always discuss the effect it creates. Reread 'Mother, any distance' and consider the effect of 'leaving' (6), 'feeding' and 'unreeling' (7) in verse five.

LINKS BETWEEN POEMS

As stated on the previous page, theoretically you should be ready to compare/contrast the given poem with any other poem in the cluster, but it might be useful to prepare a few combinations. As you read, consider whether other poems share or contrast with the same features as those highlighted in bold. Here are some possible links:

Poem	Thematic or contextual links	Voice, form/structure or technique links
'When We Two Parted'	'Neutral Tones' also explores deception, but unlike 'When We Two Parted' uses **nature imagery** to convey themes.	'Neutral Tones' also has a male voice that explores female deception, and **no female voice replies**.
'Love's Philosophy'	'Sonnet 29 – "I think of thee!"' also **celebrates love**. However, 'Love's Philosophy' is a lyric poem from the **Romantic movement**.	'Sonnet 29 – "I think of thee!"' also uses nature imagery to convey feelings.
'Porphyria's Lover'	'The Farmer's Bride' also depicts a **failed relationship**, but 'Porphyria's Lover' involves murder.	There is **no closure** in either poem. The reader of 'The Farmer's Bride' suspects something sinister may happen. 'Porphyria's Lover' ends as the speaker waits for God to speak.
'Sonnet 29 – "I think of thee!"'	Like 'Porphyria's Lover', it has a **mid-nineteenth century setting**.	Both use **traditional verse forms**. 'Sonnet 29 – "I think of thee!"' is a sonnet, while 'Porphyria's Lover' is a dramatic monologue.
'Neutral Tones'	'Follower' also shows **how past experience affects the present**.	Both have a **first person speaker**, but the mood in 'Neutral Tones' is resigned and bitter, while in 'Follower' it is poignant.
'Letters from Yorkshire'	'Walking Away' also depicts strong ties, despite **separation**.	Both use nature imagery and both include images of birds, distance and **connotations** of flight.
'The Farmer's Bride'	'Singh Song!' and 'The Farmer's Bride' depict marriages, but have contrasting depictions of the wives and husbands.	'Singh Song!' and 'The Farmer's Bride' use **dialect** to create authenticity.

continued on page 86

'Walking Away'	'Sonnet 29 – "I think of thee!"' also explores separation, but the poems' different styles reflect their different contexts. 'Walking Away' is a **modern poem**, while 'Sonnet 29 – "I think of thee!"' is mid nineteenth century.	'Sonnet 29 – "I think of thee!"' has the same **metre**, iambic pentameter. Both speakers also find an answer to their dilemmas, a complete one in 'Sonnet 29 – "I think of thee!"'; a poignant one in 'Walking Away'.
'Eden Rock'	'Climbing My Grandfather' also examines **the nature of kinship and intimacy** through potent early memories.	Both poems **use form to highlight meaning**. 'Eden Rock' sets the last line apart for emphasis. The shape of 'Climbing My Grandfather' mimics the face of a mountain or cliff.
'Follower'	'Eden Rock' also shares the theme of **parental bonds** and also explores potent **childhood memories**.	Both poems use **alliteration**, and in particular there are numerous examples of **sibilance**.
'Mother, any distance'	Letters from Yorkshire' like 'Mother, any distance' explores the theme of **separation**. In the former there is a struggle to break parental bonds. In the latter there is communication over distance.	In 'Mother, any distance' the speaker addresses the mother in the **second person**. In 'Letters from Yorkshire' the speaker shifts from addressing the reader, to the friend in the second person.
'Before You Were Mine'	Both 'Before You Were Mine' and 'Mother, any distance' focus on the mother in the mother/child relationship. However, in the former the speaker portrays the mother with affection; in the latter, with resentment.	Both poems use **colloquial** language for effects, and 'Before You Were Mine' uses a Northern/Gaelic **vernacular**.
'Winter Swans'	'When We Two Parted' also explores the nature of estrangement, but the split is final. In 'Winter Swans' the focus is on reconciliation.	'When We Two Parted' is marked by its **passionate voice**. By contrast, the voice in 'Winter Swans' has a quiet intensity.
'Singh Song!'	'Before You Were Mine' also explores **cultural contexts** and urban settings.	Both speakers have strong **voices that are foregrounded**.
'Climbing My Grandfather'	'Mother, any distance' also explores **family ties**, through a mother/son relationship rather than a grandfather/grandson one.	'Mother, any distance', like 'Climbing My Grandfather', uses **extended metaphors**.

EXPLORING IDEAS AND ISSUES IN BOTH POEMS

The main focus for the exam question will be some sort of issue, idea or attitude related to the overall theme of *Love and Relationships*. So, how might you respond to this? You might explore connections related to:

1 The **context and background** of the issue. For example, is there a tradition of poetry about romantic love, unrequited love or family bonds? If so, how might the issue have been dealt with differently over time? What seems to be the attitude to it in your two poems? Are there any issues around the position of women, multiculturalism or changing social attitudes connected with it?

TOP TIP (A01)

There is more detail on contextual issues in **Part Three** of this Study Guide.

Example: Read one student's paragraph about one poem in relation to the presentation of ideas about the passing of time. In this paragraph the student addresses context.

> 'Neutral Tones' was written in 1867, when Hardy was still a young man of twenty-seven, well before he met his first wife, but it is a painful, bitter account. The speaker looks back on a lovers' meeting on a cold 'winter's day' that reflects the relationship. The voice suggests that the speaker is an experienced older man – 'Since then' implies the passing of time. It is a voice that seems to have grown cynical, having learned 'keen lessons' about how 'love deceives'. It suggests that not only did Hardy have a powerful imagination (whether or not he drew on his own experience) but also that his view of love was one of loss and sadness, even when young. Hardy's poems of love are marked by their feelings of sorrow at whatever age he wrote them.

2 The **voice**, **viewpoint** and **perspective** of each speaker and how they are similar or different. For example, is a particular speaker writing 'in the moment', while the other is reflecting from a distance or at an older age? Does the speaker use everyday language that is modern or in the recent past, or is the language archaic? Does the speaker use dialect? Is the dialect contemporary or does it seem to be from another time?

Example: Read one student's paragraph writing about a chosen second poem in relation to ideas about parental bonds.

> In 'Before You Were Mine' the speaker in the poem imagines her mother's early life before the speaker was born, and so is thinking about the gap of history between them. The voice has a mood of excitement and wonder as the speaker imagines her mother as glamorous in her 'high-heeled red shoes'. The reference to 'Marilyn' is to the star Marilyn Monroe, popular in the 1950s. Therefore, it dates the mother's teenage years in the poem to that period.

3 The **language and literary techniques/effects** in the two poems. This is a large area, but drawing out what is distinctively similar or different, perhaps in the directness of language; what words can be grouped together (such as words that all relate to 'winter'); and poems that have similar imagery, such as nature imagery, will enable you to explore parallels and divisions.

Example: Here a student comments on the effect of the seasons in 'Walking Away' and 'Eden Rock'.

'Walking Away' is set at the end of summer on 'A sunny day with leaves just turning'. The effect is to create not only the sense that there are fewer sunny days to come as autumn draws in, but also implies the loss of joy associated with the son leaving to attend a new school. So the imagery helps to create a mood of tenderness and sadness.

In contrast, 'Eden Rock' is set in what feels like the middle of summer, at picnic time. There is a strong sense of heat in the poem partly created by the imagery of the white sky 'as if lit by three suns' that reminds us of the brightness of a heatwave. The summer here is unusual. It is a memory partly created in the speaker's mind, as he imagines being a child again and meeting his parents in Paradise. So this summer image also has religious overtones.

4 The **form**, **structure** and **patterning** of the poems. What can these reveal about how the poems relate to the focus of the task? By looking at how the poems are divided and what structural characteristics they contain, you will be able to draw out key links and differences. For example, by commenting on repetition of particular words or phrases, or how a specific line is shortened, broken or repeated for effect.

Example: Here a student demonstrates real insight in contrasting the structural effect of the resolutions in 'Sonnet 29 – "I think of thee!"' and 'Winter Swans'.

In 'Sonnet 29 – "I think of thee!"' the poet has created a circular effect at the end of the sonnet as part of the structure of the poem, so that the ending returns to the beginning. The final line, 'I do not think of thee' draws the reader back to the first line of the poem, 'I think of thee' to create an antithesis. This contrary situation can be explained. A resolution has been found since the speaker no longer needs to be engulfed by thoughts of her absent lover when she can have him with her. She does not need to think of him when he is near.

Like 'Sonnet 29 "I think of thee!"', 'Winter Swans' also has a structure that reaches a resolution to the difficulties the lovers encounter, but in a different way. The distance between the lovers as they walk 'silent and apart' in the early verses of the poem is mended by the arrival of the two swans. The birds are always together, 'in unison', and provide an example for the lovers. When the lovers come together again it is expressed as a couplet, a rhyme pattern that is often used at the end of love poems to signify closure and resolution.

THE LANGUAGE OF EXPLORATION, COMPARISON AND CONTRAST

You will probably be familiar with the range of useful connectives and other words or phrases that can help you to explain ideas, draw links or explore contrasts in your responses, but here is a grid containing some key terms. Bear in mind that these are just as useful for developing an argument about one poem as they are for two.

TOP TIP (A01)

Practise writing paragraphs on individual points, correctly using words or phrases from the grid below.

Sequencing ideas	Developing an idea	Illustrating	Cause and effect
firstly, to start with, initially secondly, next, then, later finally, in conclusion	as well as and also too furthermore moreover in addition	for example such as for instance as shown by in this way	so because therefore thus hence consequently as a result of leading to
Comparing similarities	**Qualifying**	**Contrasting**	**Emphasising**
both equally in the same way similarly likewise as	however yet although unless except if apart from despite	in contrast on the other hand whereas instead of alternatively otherwise unlike	indeed notably above all especially particularly most of all

REVISION FOCUS: EXPLORATION, COMPARISON AND CONTRAST

Go back to the student paragraphs on pages 87 and 88. Can you spot any of the key terms above being used? Could you replace any with alternatives from the grid?

PROGRESS CHECK

GOOD PROGRESS

I can:
- Recognise and explain clearly similarities and differences between the two poems ☐
- Justify my comments with relevant evidence and accurate terminology. ☐

EXCELLENT PROGRESS

I can:
- Interpret the writers' methods and approaches to draw out insights about the two poems ☐
- Select apt and precise evidence to support my points and use subject terminology thoughtfully. ☐

THE EXAM

As well as the questions based on the *Love and Relationships* cluster of poems from the Anthology you have been given, you will also have to answer questions in the exam on two **new** poems which you haven't seen before.

This is often referred to as the 'Unseen' element of the exam, and it comes in Section C, after you have answered the question on the poems from the Anthology cluster (in Section B).

In **Section C**, you will be:

- given an 'unseen' poem printed in the exam paper
- asked to answer a single essay question on this poem (worth 24 marks), focused on how the poet presents certain ideas
- given a second 'unseen' poem (also printed on your exam paper)
- asked to answer a comparative question based on links between the second and first poem (worth 8 marks).

So, you will have **two** 'unseen' poems to answer on, with most of the available marks for the first question on the first poem on its own.

ASSESSMENT

This part of the exam assesses **Assessment Objective 1** (response to ideas, supported by evidence) and **Assessment Objective 2** (writers' effects – language, form and structure) equally, with 50% of the marks for each.

QUESTION TYPES

The **first question** will ask you something about the way the poet has presented particular ideas, for example:

'How does the poet present the speaker's feelings about his father?' or 'How does the poet present ideas about the power of nature?'

The **second question** will ask you to compare the first and second poems in some way, for example:

'In both poems the speakers describe feelings about leaving home. What are the similarities and/or differences between the ways the poets present those feelings?'

TYPES OR STYLES OF POEM

There is no one set style or predictable 'type' of poem you will be given, so you need to prepare for every eventuality. However, part of the skill being assessed is for you to be able to recognise what is **distinctive** about the poem, what the poet is saying, and how he or she says it – its flavour, if you like – and the ingredients that make up the recipe.

TOP TIP (A01)

The total marks for these two questions is **32**, which is slightly more than for the Section B question on the cluster, so make sure you give **at least the same amount of time**, if not slightly more, for the 'unseens' – so, **at least 45 minutes.**

HOW TO APPROACH THE FIRST 'UNSEEN' POEM QUESTION

It is perfectly normal to see an 'unseen' poem as a blur of words on the page, and feel it's a difficult puzzle, like an equation, you have to solve. However, it doesn't need to be like this! It is important that you:

- approach the poem with an open mind, looking to enjoy exploring its language and ideas
- have some key strategies ready which you can quickly put into action
- stick to time limits for note-making and annotations, and leave yourself enough time to write your answer.

STAGE 1: READ THE POEM AND THE QUESTION

- First read the poem through and try to grasp what the poem is broadly about (such as love, friendship or other themes).
- Read the poem again, keeping the exam question in mind.
- Reread any part of the poem if you are uncertain about its meaning. Try to understand it in relation to what the poem is broadly about.

STAGE 2: MAKE NOTES AND ANNOTATIONS ON THE PAGE

- Underline key words in the poem.
- Underline any images/techniques that seem to help you answer the question.
- Note any special features (such as layout) that seem to enhance the meaning in relation to the question.
- Jot down some short questions or notes to help you (for example, *Images that reinforce feelings such as romance or sorrow. Alliteration that reinforces feelings*).

STAGE 3: USE YOUR NOTES AND ANNOTATIONS TO HELP YOU WRITE YOUR RESPONSE

Include:

- The poem's overall 'story' and how it relates to the focus of the task
- The voice and perspective of the speaker, if relevant
- How the structure contributes to the effect
- How the language techniques contribute to the effect

Now turn over the page to look at how to approach a typical task.

> **TOP TIP** (A01)
>
> Try to spend **30 to 35 minutes** on the **first question**. This should be enough for you to read, make notes and respond.

Question: How does the poet present the **narrator's feelings** about **humans and nature** in this poem?

This suggests you should be looking for:

- a viewpoint or emotions about humans' relationship with the natural world
- positive or negative language or descriptions
- what sort of 'story', if any, is told about nature and what is happening/ has happened.

Now look at how the 'unseen' poem has been annotated:

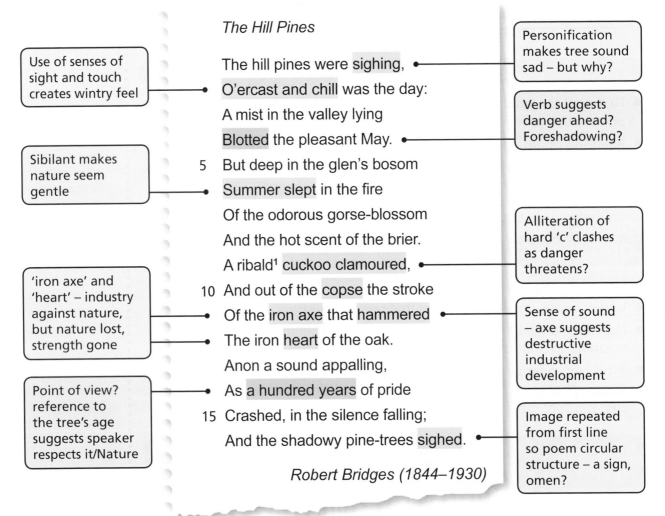

The Hill Pines

The hill pines were sighing,
O'ercast and chill was the day:
A mist in the valley lying
Blotted the pleasant May.
5 But deep in the glen's bosom
Summer slept in the fire
Of the odorous gorse-blossom
And the hot scent of the brier.
A ribald[1] cuckoo clamoured,
10 And out of the copse the stroke
Of the iron axe that hammered
The iron heart of the oak.
Anon a sound appalling,
As a hundred years of pride
15 Crashed, in the silence falling;
And the shadowy pine-trees sighed.

Robert Bridges (1844–1930)

Annotations:

- Use of senses of sight and touch creates wintry feel
- Sibilant makes nature seem gentle
- 'iron axe' and 'heart' – industry against nature, but nature lost, strength gone
- Point of view? reference to the tree's age suggests speaker respects it/Nature
- Personification makes tree sound sad – but why?
- Verb suggests danger ahead? Foreshadowing?
- Alliteration of hard 'c' clashes as danger threatens?
- Sense of sound – axe suggests destructive industrial development
- Image repeated from first line so poem circular structure – a sign, omen?

Glossary

[1] ribald = rude or indecent

WHAT ARE THE OVERALL CONCLUSIONS?

For higher marks examiners will be looking to see if you can arrive at a 'conceptualisation' – a sort of whole picture of the poem – which you can explain consistently. For example, the student might say, based on his/her annotations that:

The poet personifies the pines so that the reader feels close to them, and uses alliteration to create the effect that nature is benign. By contrast the axe is brutal and represents industrial expansion. The felling of the tree is seen as destructive of nature as a whole.

WRITING A RESPONSE

Here is one possible way of structuring your response:

Paragraph	Point
Opening paragraph	Establish quickly and clearly the 'story' the poem tells. For example: *The narrator of 'The Hill Pines' describes a situation in which an old oak tree is felled, and the response of the other trees – the pines of the title – to it. Through the descriptions, we can infer what the poet thinks of the action.*
Paragraphs 2–4	Introduce detailed points related to 'man and nature': • the tree represents nature and nature is benign • humans threaten nature through industrial development • humans are therefore destructive.
Paragraphs 5–6	Add a couple of further ideas: • there is foreshadowing in the first verse – suggesting danger ahead • the last line echoes the first (a circular poem).
Concluding paragraph	Sum up concisely – don't list all the ideas again. For example: *The poet presents the reader with a depiction of nature under threat from industrial development. The last line of the poem echoes the first line and also the title, so the poem is circular. Because we return to the beginning, the suggestion is that the whole forest could be cleared, and this in turn emphasises how humans destroy nature.*

HOW TO APPROACH THE SECOND 'UNSEEN' POEM QUESTION

You have fewer marks for the comparison question, so:

- Read through the second poem and with the question task in mind, make very brief notes around the poem (perhaps 2 minutes of quick annotation).
- Decide the main points of comparison and difference.
- Write your response.

Try to allow **15 to 20 minutes** for this, the **second question**. Your teacher may advise you to spend more or less time on the 'unseen' and Anthology cluster questions depending on your own strengths and weaknesses, so make sure you check what their advice is too.

TOP TIP A01

For further help with comparing poems, turn to **Part Five** of this Study Guide. That section gives advice on comparing poems in the Anthology cluster, but you can apply the same skills when comparing 'unseen' poems too.

PRACTICE TASK 1

Now, complete this two-part Practice task featuring two 'unseen' poems, using the process on pages 91–3. Write two full-length responses and then use the Mark scheme on pages 117–18 to assess your work.

> **Question 1:** How does the poet present the speaker's feelings about war in this poem? (24 marks)

1 Underline the key words in the title.

2 Read the poem through once, without making notes but with the focus of the task in the back of your mind.

3 Read it again, making notes, annotations and highlights around it.

4 Write your response.

An Irish Airman Foresees His Death

I know that I shall meet my fate
Somewhere among the clouds above;
Those that I fight I do not hate
5   Those that I guard I do not love;
My country is Kiltartan Cross,¹
My countrymen Kiltartan's poor,
No likely end could bring them loss
Or leave them happier than before.
10   Nor law, nor duty bade me fight,
Nor public man, nor cheering crowds,
A lonely impulse of delight
Drove to this tumult in the clouds;
I balanced all, brought all to mind,
15   The years to come seemed waste of breath,
A waste of breath the years behind
In balance with this life, this death.

                    W. B. Yeats (1865–1939)

Glossary

¹ Kiltartan Cross = a village in Ireland

Now read the second poem:

Horses Aboard

Horses in horse cloths stand in a row

On board the huge ship that as last lets go:

Whither are they sailing? They do not know,

Nor what for, nor how. –

5   They are horses of war,

And are going to where there is fighting afar;

But they gaze through their eye-holes unwitting they are,

And that in some wilderness, gaunt and ghast,[1]

Their bones will bleach ere a year has passed,

10   And the item be as 'war-waste' classed. –

And when the band booms, and the folk say 'Good bye!'

And the shore slides astern, they appear wrenched awry

From the scheme Nature planned for them – wondering why.

Thomas Hardy (1840–1928)

Glossary

[1] ghast = an older form of 'ghastly'

Question 2: In both poems, 'An Irish Airman Foresees His Death' and 'Horses Aboard', the speakers discuss the impact of war on ordinary people or animals. What are the similarities/differences between the ways the poets present these ideas? (8 marks)

1 Quickly read the second poem and question, and make very brief notes.

2 Write your comparison – three to four paragraphs on similarities and one on differences.

PRACTICE TASK 2

Now complete this further 'unseen' two-part practice task. Write two full-length responses and then use the Mark scheme on pages 117–18 to assess your work.

Question 1: How does the poet present ideas about memory and the past in this poem? (24 marks)

I Remember, I Remember

I remember, I remember
The house where I was born,
The little window where the sun
Came peeping in at morn;
5   He never came a wink too soon
Nor brought too long a day;
But now, I often wish the night
Had borne my breath away.

I remember, I remember
10 The roses red and white,
The violets and the lily cups—
Those flowers made of light!
The lilacs where the robin built,
And where my brother set
15 The laburnum on his birthday,—
The tree is living yet!

I remember, I remember
Where I was used to swing,
And thought the air must rush as fresh
20 To swallows on the wing;
My spirit flew in feathers then
That is so heavy now,
The summer pools could hardly cool
The fever on my brow.

25 I remember, I remember
The fir-trees dark and high;
I used to think their slender tops
Were close against the sky:
It was a childish ignorance,
30 But now 'tis little joy
To know I'm farther off from Heaven
Than when I was a boy.

Thomas Hood (1799–1845)

Piano

Softly, in the dusk, a woman is singing to me;
Taking me back down the vista of years, till I see
A child sitting under the piano, in the boom of the tingling strings
And pressing the small, poised feet of a mother who smiles as she sings.

5   In spite of myself, the insidious mastery of song
Betrays me back, till the heart of me weeps to belong
To the old Sunday evenings at home, with winter outside
And hymns in the cosy parlour, the tinkling piano our guide.

So now it is vain for the singer to burst into clamour
10   With the great black piano appassionato. The glamour
Of childish days is upon me, my manhood is cast
Down in the flood of remembrance, I weep like a child for the past.

D. H. Lawrence (1885–1930)

Question 2: In both poems, 'I Remember, I Remember' and 'The Piano', the speakers remember what it was like to be a child. What are the similarities/differences between the ways the poets present ideas about childhood? (8 marks)

PROGRESS CHECK

GOOD PROGRESS

I can:

● Explain the methods of the writer of the first 'unseen' poem clearly using a range of references ☐

● Recognise and explain clearly similarities and differences between the two 'unseen' poems. ☐

EXCELLENT PROGRESS

I can:

● Draw out and interpret the methods and approaches of the writer of the first 'unseen' poem, selecting apt and precise evidence ☐

● Make a convincing comparison between the two 'unseen' poems, with well-judged analysis. ☐

UNDERSTANDING THE QUESTION

In **Section B** of the exam, you will:

- be given one poem from the cluster, which will be printed on your exam paper

  and

- be asked to compare it with another poem of your choice from the cluster, by answering one question on an aspect common to the given poem and the one of your choice.

The question is worth **30 marks**, and examines **AOs 1, 2 and 3**, with **80%** of marks available for **AOs 1 and 2**. This does not mean you should ignore AO3 (contextual factors or perspectives), but do not write too much about it! You will have approximately 45 minutes to answer the question.

TYPICAL QUESTIONS

In your exam, a typical question will look like this:

> How does the poet present failed relationships in 'Neutral Tones'? Compare with one other poem of your choice from the collection.

BREAK DOWN THE QUESTION

Pick out the key words or phrases. For example:

How does the **poet present failed relationships** in '**Neutral Tones**'? **Compare** with **one other poem** of your choice from the collection.

What does this tell you?

Write about:

- Attitudes to failed relationships
- How the poets present these attitudes through the way they write

PLANNING YOUR ANSWER

Bearing in mind you have just 45 minutes (or less if you want to spend more time on **Section A** or **C**), you will need to respond swiftly and efficiently. This means that you should spend no more than 5 minutes planning – remember, you will already know the poems well.

STAGE 1: SELECTING POEMS FOR COMPARISON

Your teacher may have already suggested possible poems to compare 'Neutral Tones' with, but here are a few ideas.

- 'The Farmer's Bride' – the poet presents a failed marriage, the theme is unrequited love
- 'When We Two Parted' – the poet presents an illicit love that has failed and in which the speaker has been deceived by his lover

STAGE 2: ANNOTATING THE GIVEN POEM AND CREATING LINKS

Let us compare 'Neutral Tones' with 'The Farmer's Bride'. Look at how one student has used the exam paper to annotate 'Neutral Tones' and make notes on 'The Farmer's Bride':

NT: Stillness

TFB: Winter landscape connotations of death. See also leaf image line 36/'Neutral Tones' line 3

NT: Long relationship

TFB: Short relationship

NT: Desire gone

TFB: Farmer's desire increases/ becomes sinister. Sense of urgency in last verse

NT: Common structure returns to beginning. Effect no hope

TFB: Contrast: poem ends on an unfinished note

NT: Personifies earth as desperate for life

TFB: No personification, but wife compared to frightened animals through images/ motif

NT: Deception

TFB: Farmer expected too much from wife? Feels deceived? Lines 2, 7, 29, 33

Neutral Tones

We stood by a pond that winter day,

And the sun was white, as though chidden of God,

And a few leaves lay on the starving sod;

They had fallen from an ash, and were grey.

5 Your eyes on me were as eyes that rove

Over tedious riddles of years ago;

And some words played between us to and fro

On which lost the more by our love.

The smile on your mouth was the deadest thing

10 Alive enough to have strength to die;

And a grin of bitterness swept thereby

Like an ominous bird a-wing …

Since then, keen lessons that love deceives,

And wrings with wrong, have shaped to me

15 Your face, and the God curst sun, and a tree,

And a pond edged with greyish leaves.

Thomas Hardy (1840–1928)

Key things to compare	Key things to contrast
• Both have failed relationships, speakers feel deceived • Both told through voice of male speaker. Other person (women) have no voice • Both have nature imagery conveying death/dying through winter	• NT speaker's desire dead/TFB desire increases • Thoughts only in NT, no events. TFB tells a narrative • NT circular ending. Repetition suggests no hope for relationship. TFB ends on unfinished note: what might happen next?

STAGE 3: WRITING YOUR RESPONSE

First section of response: Three or four points on **Poem A**, perhaps on **voice, viewpoint** and **context**, supported by reference to the **language**.

- 'Neutral Tones' has a bleak winter setting, in which the earth, 'the starving sod' (3) is personified to convey the speaker's dead relationship with the other person.
- We only have the speaker's viewpoint of the relationship, which focuses on the other person. Frequent use of second person in stanzas 3, 4, 5, lines 5, 9, 15.
- The structure of the poem is circular, the end returns to the beginning; a common structure to show repetition of feelings, and here it shows that the relationship cannot flourish.

Second section of response: Bringing in **Poem B**, perhaps picking up **similarities** and **differences** at this point.

- 'The Farmer's Bride' also includes a bleak winter setting in stanza 5, where a single 'leaf in the still air falls slowly down' (36), much like the leaf image in 'Neutral Tones'. Both images of winter, when nothing grows, convey the bleakness of the relationship. The stillness suggests lack of energy and passion.
- 'The Farmer's Bride' is spoken by a male voice, and this is the only point of view the reader has. Similarly in 'Neutral Tones'. So we do not know what the female voice thinks. For example, why is the young wife so determined to keep 'men-folk' (24) at a distance?
- One important difference in the two poems is the increase and decrease in passion. At the end of 'The Farmer's Bride' the farmer yearns for 'the soft young down' (45) of his wife, implying impatience as well as passion. In 'Neutral Tones' the woman's face is compared to the 'God-curst sun' (15). A curse suggests the relationship is ill-fated.

Third section of response: One to two points **developing** or **adding to** earlier ideas on **either of the two poems**.

- There are implications that the farmer feels deceived by his bride, particularly in the line 'and 'twasn't a woman' (7), as though the bride, as a woman, however young, should have known what to expect from marriage. In 'Neutral Tones' the speaker also feels 'that love deceives' (13), perhaps love itself rather than the other person only. Love's early promises do not seem to have been fulfilled.

Final section: Concluding paragraph

- Both poems deal with failed relationships and speakers who are disappointed by love or marriage.
- An important difference between the two poems is in their conclusions. In 'Neutral Tones' the ending, which returns to the thoughts and images at the beginning of the poem, suggests there is no hope for the relationship. In contrast, 'The Farmer's Bride' has no closure insofar as the reader expects something more sinister to happen in the relationship.

TOP TIP (A01)

You may not have time to write a detailed plan, but this is one suggested structure for your response, which involves writing about the first poem, then bringing in the second, but making a clear link to the first when you do so.

TOP TIP (A01)

There are several ways to structure a response: you could write a paragraph about Poem A, then one on Poem B, then one on Poem A, then again Poem B, and so on, but this may end up sounding a little mechanical. Alternatively, *within* paragraphs you could move between both poems, but you will need to be confident you can do this fluently and coherently.

RESPONDING TO WRITERS' EFFECTS

The two most important assessment objectives are **AO1** and **AO2**. They are about *what* poets do (the choices they make, and the effects these create), *what* your ideas are (your analysis and interpretation) and *how* you write about them (how well you explain your ideas).

ASSESSMENT OBJECTIVE 1 (AO1)

What does it say?	What does it mean?	Dos and don'ts
Read, understand and respond to texts. Students should be able to: ● Maintain a critical style and develop an informed personal response ● Use textual references, including quotations, to support and illustrate interpretations	You must: ● Use some of the literary terms you have learned (correctly!) ● Write in a professional way (not a sloppy, chatty way) ● Show that you have thought for yourself ● Back up your ideas with examples, including quotations	**Don't write …** *The bride in 'A Farmer's Bride' is like an animal or a bird.* **Do write …** *Mew's depiction of the young bride is that of a timid creature, 'shy as a leveret' or happy to 'chat' to 'birds and rabbits'. The comparison with a young hare and wild birds suggests that she is an unapproachable young woman, one who is ill at ease in the human world, but feels at home in the natural world.*

IMPROVING YOUR CRITICAL STYLE

Use a variety of words and phrases to show effects:

The poet *suggests …, conveys …, implies …, presents how …, explores …, demonstrates …, describes how …, shows how …*
I/we (as readers) *infer …, recognise …, understand …, question …, see …, are given …, reflect …*

For example, look at these two alternative paragraphs by different students about the speaker in 'Sonnet 29 – "I think of thee!"'. Note the difference in the quality of expression.

Student A:

This makes it seem as if Barrett Browning is speaking

Repetitive – better to use an alternative

Elizabeth Barrett Browning says that her thoughts are everywhere like thoughts sometimes are. She writes of 'Thoughts that 'twine and bud/About thee' and of 'wild vines, about a tree'. This shows that the speaker clings to her lover and cannot stop thinking about him. This shows that she is very much attached to her lover.

Chatty, informal and vague

Unclear whether 'She' refers to Barrett Browning or the speaker

Student B:

> **Fits with the idea of the overall way the speaker is shown**

> **Good variety of vocabulary**

> **Looks beyond the obvious and infers meaning with personal interpretation**

Elizabeth Barrett Browning presents the speaker in the first quatrain as someone whose thoughts of love overwhelm her. She demonstrates the speaker's feelings as thoughts that 'twine and bud' about her like 'wild vines about a tree'. The poet seems to be presenting the lover as the tree, since the image 'straggling green which hides the tree' implies that the speaker's thoughts are so overpowering that they blot out the image of her lover in her mind's eye.

> **Clear and precise language**

> **Phrase allows the student to explore the idea rather than state it as fact**

ASSESSMENT OBJECTIVE 2   (A02)

What does it say?	What does it mean?	Dos and don'ts
Analyse the language, form and structure used by the poet to create meanings and effects, using relevant subject terminology where appropriate.	• 'Analyse' – comment **in detail** on **particular aspects** of the poem or language • 'Language' – what the poet writes and how they say it • 'Form' – **how** the poem is told (e.g. how the poem is laid out using different shapes or verse forms such as sonnet, quatrains, tercets • 'Structure' – the **order** in which events are revealed, or in which characters appear, or descriptions are presented • 'Create meaning' – what can we, as readers, **infer** from what the poet tells us? What is **implied** by particular descriptions, or events? • 'Subject terminology' – **words** you should use when writing about poetry, such as 'imagery', 'metaphor' 'irony' 'symbol' 'setting', etc.	**Don't write …** *The writing is very sad in this bit of the poem because you can see how the farmer feels unhappy.* **Do write …** *Mew **conveys** the Farmer's **mood** in the winter **setting** through the way the 'magpie's spotted feathers lie/On the black earth spread white with rime'. The overall **image** of winter seems to reflect the farmer's sorrow at the lack of intimacy in his marriage.*

IMPLICATIONS, INFERENCES AND INTERPRETATIONS

- The best analysis focuses on specific ideas or events, or uses of language, and thinks about what is **implied**.

- This means drawing **inferences**. From the farmer's account in 'The Farmer's Bride' the farmer seems to be the wronged party. It is he who complains about his young wife's lack of responsiveness, and though he acknowledges in the opening of the poem that his bride was too young, and that there was no courtship, he dismisses it as unimportant. So what does it reveal about his attitude to marriage? How does he think his wife should be treated? What position does he think his wife should have in the marriage?

- From the inferences you make across the poem as a whole, you can arrive at your own **interpretation** – a sense of the bigger picture, a wider evaluation of a speaker, relationship or idea.

USING QUOTATIONS

One of the secrets of success in writing exam essays is to use quotations **effectively**. There are five basic principles:

1 Only quote what is most useful.

2 Do not use a quotation that repeats what you have just written.

3 Put quotation marks, i.e. '', around the quotation.

4 Write the quotation exactly as it appears in the original.

5 Use the quotation so that it fits neatly into your sentence.

EXAM FOCUS: USING QUOTATIONS

Quotations should be used to develop the line of thought in your essay, and to 'zoom in' on key details, such as language choices. The mid-level example below shows a clear and effective way of doing this:

> **Makes a clear point**
>
> **Explains the effect of the quotation**
>
> Elizabeth Barrett Browning presents the lover as someone who is strong and that the speaker thinks about all the time. The speaker says, 'be it understood/I will not have my thoughts instead of thee/Who art dearer, better! Rather instantly/Renew thy presence'. This shows the speaker wants the lover with her instead of her thoughts.
>
> **Gives an apt quotation**

However, really **high-level responses** will go further. They will make an even more precise point, support it with a more well-chosen quotation, focus on particular word or phrases and explain the effect or what is implied to make a wider point or draw inferences.

> **Precise point**
>
> **Language feature**
>
> Elizabeth Barrett Browning presents the speaker's view of her lover in the octave as strong, dependent; someone she is preoccupied with and wants by her side. Unable to contain her passion, she declares, 'be it understood/I will not have my thoughts instead of thee/Who art dearer, better! Rather instantly/Renew thy presence'. This marks a turn in the sonnet, a volta, and with it comes a shift in the tone of the speaker's voice as she demands her lover's presence rather than be overwhelmed with thoughts of him.
>
> **Precise quotation**
>
> **Explanation/ implication/effect**
>
> **Further development/link**

ANNOTATED SAMPLE ANSWERS

This section will provide you with three **sample responses**, one at a **mid** level, one at a **good** level, and one at a **very high** level.

> **Question:** Compare how poets present ideas about failed relationships in 'Porphyria's Lover' and one other poem from the collection you have studied.

SAMPLE ANSWER 1

A02 Needs to be more precise about form. Should mention dramatic monologue and the speaker as a persona

'Porphyria's Lover' is like a narrative and the story is about a failed relationship, which has broken down because the person in the story, called the speaker, has murdered his lover. The speaker's lover has come to visit him through the 'sullen wind' to the cottage. He does not seem well, so she looks after him by making up the fire, but then when she is sitting by him quietly, he wraps her hair around her throat 'three times' and strangles her. It comes as a bit of a shock to the reader. The reason why is because we are not expecting it. This shows the poet's skill at creating surprise. It is not easy to work out why the speaker murdered Porphyria. He is out of touch with reality, so perhaps he did not know what he was doing.

A01 Quotation embedded successfully in the sentence

A01 Describes the effect on the reader, but language too informal and no investigation of how the poet achieves surprise

A02 Useful connective to compare two situations

On the other hand, he is happy after he has committed the murder because he thinks that he has 'gained' Porphyria. So perhaps he thinks that they can 'sit together' without anything changing between them and so nobody else can have Porphyria. At the end of the poem he seems to be waiting for God to say something. The reader does not know why. Perhaps the speaker thinks he is to be punished, but so far 'God has not said a word!'. The whole poem is like a Gothic story, or a horror story.

A01 A good attempt at analysis, but needs to be supported with evidence

A03 Useful reference to the Gothic but needs to be discussed within the paragraph and not simply added on

A01 Makes a comparison, but needs to develop the comment on the difference between the two relationships

The Farmer's Bride is also about a failed relationship, but it is not quite the same as 'Porphyria's Lover'.

In this poem Charlotte Mew tells us a narrative about a farmer who has married a very young wife. She does not love the farmer and is afraid of men in general. The poet uses a simile 'Like the shut of a winter's day' to show the wife's fear. She would rather be with the animals in the farm and the poet compares her to a wild animal, 'shy as a leveret', which is

A02 Good understanding of technique and quotation embedded in the sentence mentioned

A01 Good point and quotation but needs to expand on why it is like a black and white film

a young hare. When the wife runs away, they catch her and lock her up, which shows us that at that time you could do such a thing to women. As the poem moves along, it becomes autumn, then winter and the poet uses nature imagery, a bit like in 'Porphyria's Lover', but there's no storm. In this poem there is brown, grey and a colourless kind of tone along with a 'magpie's spotted feather' on the earth with white frost. So it is like a black and white film, gloomy. Also 'berries redden', which I suppose is holly, because it reminds the farmer of Christmas and having no children. It makes the reader feel sorry for the farmer.

A01 Language too informal

At the end of the poem the farmer is aware that his wife is nearby, 'but a stair/Betwixt us'. He imagines her lying in her bed and thinks in particular about her hair, so his desire becomes greater. It makes the reader feel nervous. We worry about what the farmer could easily do.

A01 Shows a sound understanding of the feeling expressed at the end of the poem

MID LEVEL

Comment

There is an understanding of both narratives and events and also some grasp of hidden meanings, but there needs to be more comparison of the similarities and differences between the poems. There also needs to be more investigation into why the poet chooses particular techniques, especially across theme, language and form and the effects they create. The reference to the Gothic context should be developed to include specific evidence from the poem. Paragraphs are used but vocabulary needs to widen and informal language be avoided.

For a Good Level:

- Show how the poet creates effects by explaining how the reader is affected when the poet uses a particular technique.
- Make more comparisons between the poems.
- Learn to develop a critical style. Avoid informal language and draw on a wider range of vocabulary.
- Investigate the context of the poems, such as the period in which the poem was written (historical context) any references to the culture (cultural context) and any biographical details that are hinted at or revealed in the poem.

SAMPLE ANSWER 2

A02 A sound introduction that refers to poem's storyline and form

A03 A sound reference to the Gothic context

A01 Draws neatly to a conclusion, but greater exploration of the speaker's motives or condition would have been useful.

A01 Comparison made but needs to be developed

'Porphyria's Lover' is both a narrative and a dramatic monologue and it tells the story of a strange relationship between the speaker and his lover that ends when he murders her. Browning presents a stormy evening in a rural setting. The wind is an example of pathetic fallacy because it has human feelings. It is described as 'sullen' because it tears the trees and does its best 'to vex the lake'. The violent stormy night and also the isolated cottage remind us of Gothic fiction with its menacing and dramatic settings. Porphyria arrives at the cottage in the storm, where the speaker, her lover, sits quietly, 'so pale/For love of her'. We know she cares for him because she banks up the fire in the 'cheerless grate' to warm him. She sits beside him, and the speaker, without any indication of what is to come, winds Porphyria's 'yellow hair' around her throat and strangles her. The effect on the reader is dramatic. There has been no quarrel or suggestion of violence. It is a cold action. Browning has created this mood for a purpose. It shows how unbalanced the speaker is. After Porphyria is dead the speaker gives her a 'burning kiss'. This image is also very disturbing, since she is a corpse and he shows more passion for her than when she was alive. At the end of the poem the speaker sits with Porphyria into the night, happy that she is dead and that he has her all to himself. The ending is a puzzle because he seems to think being dead is what Porphyria wanted, that it was her 'one wish'. He is also waiting for God to speak, but what God is to say we are not told.

'Neutral Tones' by Thomas Hardy also has the theme of a failed relationship, like 'Porphyria's Lover', but it is a relationship that has gone on for a long time because the speaker talks about 'years ago'. It sounds like a marriage, but we do not know that. Unlike 'Porphyria's Lover' it is not a narrative poem, because there are no events. Everything takes place by a pond. Hardy begins the poem with a description of the pond in winter. There are a few grey leaves, which have fallen from an 'ash' tree, and the earth is 'starving'. The sun is also white rather than yellow, as you get sometimes in winter. Hardy has used language to create images in which everything seems dead, and we know from the mood before we get to verse two that this unhappy place must be connected to the relationship. In 'Porphyria's Lover' nature was angry.

A01 Technique highlighted, but points not relevant unless the connection between the setting and the failed relationship (theme) is shown

A01 Quotation successfully embedded in the sentence

A02 Identifies a literary technique and shows how the poet uses it to create effects

A02 Shows how the poet uses techniques to create effects

A01

> Useful conjunctive adverb to qualify a point

However, Hardy is using nature imagery to show death, that the relationship is dead. The smile on the face of the other person with the speaker is the 'deadest thing', for example, and there is bitterness in her face too. Browning uses a simile to describe her grin, which is 'like an ominous bird a-wing', and which sounds like a warning and is certainly not very loving. In the last verse we realise that the speaker is also bitter or at least very cold about the relationship because he says 'that love deceives'. Why or how he does not say. We only know that the nature imagery appears again to show the relationship is over, and the voice of the speaker is so certain and depressed there seems no hope of the two coming together again.

A02

> Sound ending, but could have noted more about how the nature imagery relates to the structure of the poem

GOOD LEVEL

Comment

A sound response that shows a good grasp of the relationships the poets have presented, but a few more comparisons between the poems could have been made. Quotations are well embedded. Several literary techniques have been identified and there have been some successful attempts to explore their effects. There is a sound mention of context. Key areas such as theme, form, language and setting have been explored, but need to be developed further. The language is a little informal at times, but fluent. More variation in pace is recommended.

For a High Level:

- Make sure useful comments make satisfactory links with the question, and try to make more comparisons between the poems.
- Explore more fully the poets' techniques and effects on the reader.
- Improve the critical style. Vary pace and formality and include sophisticated vocabulary.

SAMPLE ANSWER 3

A02 Excellent introduction that combines a reference to poem's form and to nature of speaker

A03 Reference to context shows knowledge of period in which poem was written

In his poem 'Porphyria's Lover' Robert Browning presents an intimate relationship through the eyes of the speaker, a persona and well-defined character, typical of the dramatic monologue. But it is a speaker that is unreliable. This unreliability is based on his precarious mental state. Would the speaker, for example, regard his relationship with Porphyria as failed? Unlikely, although the reader certainly would, since the speaker callously murders Porphyria in a macabre fashion, reminiscent of the Victorian Gothic with which Browning is associated. In a calculated act the speaker winds Porphyria's long 'yellow hair' around her throat 'Three times' and strangles her, so that she can be his, forever. It is an act that reveals his need to control and dominate her, mirrored in the disturbing image of the 'bee' trapped in the bud's clutch. The violence is not accompanied by any change of metre or expression of anguish, and the effect is to emphasise the coldness of the act. Instead the speaker sits 'all night long' with his dead lover who as a corpse is 'perfectly pure and good', his ideal partner. He is convinced that Porphyria has been granted 'her darling one wish', that she would give up her life to make him happy, a doubtful idea.

A02 Rhetorical question that enhances style and highlights key words in exam question

A02 Shows Browning's choice of technique and its effect

A01 Important conjunctive adverb of comparison

A02 Discussion of technique and its effect, with a quotation embedded in the sentence

In contrast the speaker in 'When We Two Parted' expresses intense emotion, typical of the Romantics, of which Byron was one. Unlike Browning's distancing persona it is difficult for the reader not to feel that it is Byron who is speaking to us about his failed relationship. The effect is created partly by repetition of the misery felt. This is made clear in the noun 'shudder' that has an onomatopoeic juddering effect as though the speaker was shivering, and also in the use of the painful verb 'sever' that implies a brutal parting. The metre is strong, and confident. It reinforces the sense that the speaker's emotions are true. The occasional extra stress at the end of a line such as 'Pale grew thy cheek and cold' emphasises a darker mood through a subtle slowing of pace.

A03 Reference to the context of the poem

A02 Zooms in to analyse the effects of key words and technique

Apart from the theme of failed relationships and the regularity of rhythm and rhyme (both poems have full end rhyme) there is little that the two poems seem to have in common. However, there is one other important similarity. The reader never hears from either of the women whom the speakers depict. They remain voiceless, so we never hear their side of the story. Although Porphyria does not speak she is

A01 Use of varied sentence length for effective style to introduce important similarity between poems

not without character. There is a suggestion that she has another life beyond her relationship with the speaker. He refers to unspecified 'vainer ties', perhaps her higher social status that seems to trouble him, and this may be a possible motive for the murder. In 'When We Two Parted' the ex-lover (thought to be based on Lady Frances Wedderburn Webster) also has another life and she is accused of betrayal. 'Thy vows are all broken,/and light is thy fame' says the speaker, suggesting she is the object of gossip, but like Porphyria she cannot reply.

A03 Reference to possible biographical context

The endings of the poems could hardly be more dissimilar.

A02 Makes an important comment on the structure of the poem

In Byron's poem the last line returns to the beginning. The image 'silence and tears' is repeated, so that even after 'long years' of separation the speaker imagines that he would greet his past lover in the same way. This circular effect is part of the structure of the poem and it heightens the pathos. It leaves the reader feeling that the speaker is caught in an endless cycle of intense emotion and may never be free of regret and sorrow.

Browning's speaker is more optimistic. He waits, listening for God. Whether he imagines himself to be God or believes God's silence means approval for the murder, we do not know. From the reader's point of view the speaker is left in a terrible limbo. He seems to believe he can remain for eternity, sitting like a still life, with the dead Porphyria.

A01 Excellent concluding paragraph contrasting the poems' two endings

VERY HIGH LEVEL

Comment

This excellent essay provides a sound analysis and comparison of the two poems and addresses the exam question. There is a thorough focus on technique and the poets' effects regarding theme, form, structure and context. There is also an effort to draw out, across texts, the few similarities that exist between the poems. The range of vocabulary is sophisticated and the variety of sentence structure and pace aids the points being made. An excellent conclusion that shows real insight.

PRACTICE TASK 3

Write a full-length response to this exam-style question and then use the **Mark scheme** on pages 117–18 to assess your own response.

> **Question:** Compare how poets present ideas about family ties in 'Walking Away' and one other poem from the collection you have studied.

Stage 1: Read the given poem and choose a second poem to write about

- Find the given poem in your Anthology and read over it carefully. Underline any key words or phrases you may want to pick out, and make some quick notes on the key themes.
- Now choose a poem to compare it with. Is there a poem that discusses a similar issue or deals with the same theme in a contrasting way?
- For some suggestions for linked poems, see the grid on pages 67–8.

Stage 2: Plan your points and write your response

- Plan quickly and efficiently by using key words from the question.
- Write equally about the set poem and the other one you choose.
- Explore key points of comparison in terms of content, poetic forms and language, and context.
- Focus on the techniques the poets use and the effect of these on the reader.
- Offer your own interpretations, insights and thoughts on the poems, where possible.
- Support your ideas with relevant evidence, including quotations.

Stage 3: Check your response!

Once you've written your draft, use the **Mark scheme** on pages 117–18 to check your response. Here you'll find a list of points you could have made – these are just suggestions, but if you think you have missed something important, try to add it in to your response in your own words. You can also use the General skills section to remind you of the key criteria and to check your skills.

TOP TIP **A01**

To get you started visualise a picture of the father and the son together after the game and then imagine the father watching his son walk further and further away from him. If you wish, you can jot down two or three words that sum up how each of them feels.

LITERARY TERMS

alliteration	where the same sound is repeated in a stretch of language, usually at the beginning of words
ambiguity	when words or sentences have more than one meaning, and it is not clear which is the true interpretation
antithesis	a figure of speech in which two complete opposites are placed together but still seem to make sense
archaic	belonging to earlier or ancient times
assonance	when the same vowel sound appears in the same place in a series of words
ballad	a traditional story written in rhyme
cadence	the recurring rise and fall of the rhythms of speech; it can also refer to a rhythm that comes at the close of a line or a poem
caesura	a pause during a line of poetry
chorus	in poetry, a repeated line phrase or group of lines that is musical
colloquial	everyday speech used by people in ordinary situations
connotation	an additional meaning attached to a word in specific circumstances, i.e. what it suggests or implies
couplet	two lines of poetry that are paired
dialect	accent and vocabulary, varying by region and social background
dipodic	a light rocking metre of two feet (a unit of rhythm)
dramatic monologue	a poetic form in which a single voice addresses the reader, creating a strong sense of character
end rhyme	rhyme at the end of lines of poetry
enjambment	in poetry, when a line runs on into the next line without pause, carrying the thought with it; sometimes called a run-on line
extended metaphor	in poetry, a metaphor that continues some aspect of the image; it may continue into the next line or throughout the poem
foregrounded	a literary term used to point to a feature of the text that is emphasised
foreshadow	a hint of what is to come in a work of poetry, fiction or drama
free verse	a form of poetry; verses without regular rhythm or pattern, though they may contain some patterns, such as rhyme or repetition
genre	a distinct category in literature, such as horror stories, or historical novels
half-rhyme	where the rhyme at the end of a line has the same consonants but not the same vowel sound, so not quite a full rhyme, e.g. pet/pot
iambic pentameter	a line of poetry consisting of five iambic feet (iambic consisting of a weak syllable followed by a strong one)
iambic tetrameter	a line of poetry consisting of four iambic feet (iambic consisting of a weak syllable followed by a strong one)
idiom	an everyday expression or a common saying in a language
imagery	descriptive language that uses images to make actions, objects and characters more vivid in the reader's mind
internal rhyme	when words rhyme in the middle and at the end of a line
irony	deliberately saying one thing when another is meant, usually in a humorous, sarcastic or sometimes thoughtful way
lament	a poem expressing deep grief or sorrow

lyric	a poem, simple or complex, expressing the emotions and thoughts of the speaker and often exploring a single feeling or idea
metaphor	when one thing is used to describe another to create a striking or unusual image
metonym	a figure of speech in which the name of an idea or object is replaced with one that suggests the original (e.g. 'eyes' for sight)
metre	the pattern of stressed and unstressed syllables in a line of verse
monologue	where a single voice addresses the reader or audience
motif	a repeated theme or idea in an artistic work
narrative	a story
octave	a verse of eight lines, usually in iambic pentameter; the first eight lines of a sonnet (where it is sometimes called two quatrains)
oxymoron	a contradictory word, or a word pair or group of words that are contradictory (e.g. 'bittersweet')
paradox	a statement or group of words that contradicts itself, but has a deeper meaning (e.g. less is more)
pathetic fallacy	a technique in which human qualities are given to aspects of nature that we think of as lifeless, like the weather
persona	a character or strong voice adopted by the writer as the speaker
personificaton	the treatment or description of an object or idea as though they were human with human feelings and attributes
Petrarchan sonnet	a sonnet with an *abba, abba* rhyme scheme followed by a sestet *cdcdcd* or sometimes other rhyme
pun	similar to a word with a double meaning, a pun plays with two or more meanings in a word, usually for comic effect
quatrain	four lines of verse, can stand alone or be repeated
quintain	five lines of verse, can stand alone or be repeated
Romantic (movement)	a artistic movement that flourished in the late eighteenth century to the mid nineteenth century and valued the personal, individual, the imagination and intense feeling
rhetorical (question)	asked for effect rather than to elicit an answer
rhyme scheme	the pattern of rhyme in a poem
rhyming couplet	a couplet that rhymes
run-on line	see enjambment
sestet	a verse of six lines
sibilant	a hissing sound in speech made with an 's' or 'sh'
simile	when one thing is compared directly with another using 'like' or 'as'
sonnet	a fourteen-line verse with a rhyming couplet at the end
stanza	a group or pattern of lines forming a verse
symbol	something that represents something else, usually with meanings that are widely known (e.g. a dove as a symbol of peace)
tercet	a verse of three lines
transgression	breaking moral and social rules
voice	the speaker or narrator of a poem or work of fiction; this persona is created in the speaker's mind, though sometimes it can seem close to the poet's or writer's own voice
volta	the turn or shift in a sonnet (usually after the octave), when a second idea or mood is introduced

CHECKPOINT ANSWERS

CHECKPOINT 1, page 14

'Love's Philosophy' is:
- a belief that all things in nature are part of a pair
- expressed in human terms, the coming together of two people in love.

CHECKPOINT 2, page 17

The final line could be interpreted to suggest that:
- the speaker is waiting for God's approval, or assumes he has it because God has not spoken
- he is waiting to be punished by God for the crime
- he is questioning the existence of God
- he could be referring to himself as God (since the speaker has not 'stirred' (59) since the murder).

CHECKPOINT 3, page 24

The title 'Neutral Tones' suits the poem if we consider:
- the pale, neutral colours of the 'white' (2) sun, the 'ash' (4) tree and the 'grey' (4) leaves
- the simple quatrains and rhyme scheme (*abba*).

The title does not seems to suit:
- the resentment felt in 'a grin of bitterness' (11) in verse three
- the sense of anger felt in 'God-curst' (15) spoken in the last verse
- the suggestion in the poem that the other person is at fault, that her grin is 'like an ominous bird' (12).

CHECKPOINT 4, page 24

The meaning is ambiguous. It could imply:
- that the triviality of the conversation undermined the relationship more
- which of us was the greater loser in the relationship
- ironically that it would have been better not to have spoken at all, rather than try to connect with each other, given that there is no love at all in the relationship.

CHECKPOINT 5, page 31

The young wife seems to allow the local women to come near her, since they observe her dealings with the farm animals.
- We are told she is happy (with animals) providing men keep away.
- She sleeps alone, separated from her husband.

CHECKPOINT 6, page 34

- The poet talks of 'small' (14) 'Ordeals' (15) because they do not refer to the great difficulties that we have to bear in life, such as the death of someone close. Nonetheless, smaller events, such as the poet's parting from his son, still cause pain.

CHECKPOINT 7, page 37

- In verse one, assonance gives a subtle focus to the words 'Eden' (1), 'Tweed' (3) and 'feet' (4), where it emphasises the image of the speaker's father in his suit with his dog beside him.
- In verse two, assonance gives a subtle focus to the words 'three' (5) and 'wheat' (8), where it emphasises the image of the speaker's mother, in particular her youth and hair.
- Assonance also links both parents to 'Eden' (1).

CHECKPOINT 8, page 41

- The line 'To close one eye, stiffen my arm' (18) reveals the simple mimicry that a small child might make of the ploughman at his work.
- The line reveals that the child does not yet fully understand the skill involved in the ploughman's task.

CHECKPOINT 9, page 44

The title 'Mother, any distance' can refer to:
- the mother's need to travel to wherever her son is
- the son's awareness that his mother will come to wherever he is
- the connection between the mother and son, despite any physical distance between them.

The literal meaning of the title refers to the speaker's mother measuring every dimension in the new house.

CHECKPOINT 10, page 47

- On first reading the title 'Before You Were Mine', the reader may assume that the poem will be a love poem.
- It suggests that a lover is curious to know what the other person's life was like before they met them.
- The poem can be seen as a love poem to the speaker's mother.

CHECKPOINT 11, page 50

There are several examples of couples in the poem:
- the speaker and his partner are a couple
- 'two days of rain' (2)
- the swans are a pair
- the swans 'halved themselves in the dark water' (10)
- 'They mate for life' (13) refers to a couple
- 'our hands' (17) refers to the speaker and his partner holding hands
- 'a pair of wings' (20).

By drawing attention to couples of different kinds the central relationship between the speaker and his partner is reinforced.

CHECKPOINT 12, page 54

- By implication, the father is hardworking, is concerned about his business and appears to own several shops, because the son/speaker tells us: 'I run just one ov my daddy's shops' (1).
- The son seems to have no interest in the business and shuts the shop when he chooses. He also seems to neglect it: 'di worst Indian shop' (16).
- The poet could be making the point that we are all individuals and that a son may be very different from his father, regardless of culture.

CHECKPOINT 13, page 57

- The effect created by using the first person is intimacy. We are told what happens from a single point of view.
- The effect created by the using the present tense is immediacy. We feel we are there with the climber as he completes his journey.

CHECKPOINT 14, page 63

- The first two lines of the poem, 'The fountains mingle with the river/And the rivers with the Ocean', suggest a fluid or flexible approach to love – one that in human terms suggests that the speaker might wish to love more than one person.
- A similar effect occurs with the additional reference that the 'moonbeams' (14) in verse two 'kiss the sea' (15) (for which we can read 'Ocean' in verse one).

CHECKPOINT 15, page 71

- Italics are used when the speaker reports someone else's speech. For example when the chorus is sung by the shoppers, and when the wife's words are reported.

CHECKPOINT 16, page 72

- The fourth verse, which is a quatrain, is much shorter than the preceding verses.
- Its length (along with its pace and rhyme) helps to create a sense of the farmer's desperation at the lack of affection from his young wife.

CHECKPOINT 17, page 77

- The voice is the sensitive and troubled voice of a parent recalling the past, a particular memory of his son when he was a child.
- The poem is written in the first person, 'I'.
- The speaker is addressing the son, and because it is in the first person there is a sense of personal experience as the past is recalled.

CHECKPOINT 18, page 81

- The rhetorical question is included in verse four at the point when the farmer is increasingly troubled by his wife's behaviour and her inability to respond to him.
- The farmer knows that he means nothing to his wife, but asking the question 'But what to me?' (33) is an indirect and subtle way of making the point.

PROGRESS AND REVISION CHECK ANSWERS

PART TWO, pages 58–9

Section One: Check your knowledge

1. 'When We Two Parted'; 2. 'elm-tops' (3) and 'the lake' (4); 3. Cecil Day Lewis; 4. 'Maggie McGeeney and Jean Duff' (2); 5. The speaker as a child; 6. 'Singh Song!'; 7. 'a sweet emotion' (4); 8. 'Eden Rock', He is a terrier and his name is Jack; 9. 'Sonnet 29 – "I think of thee!"'; 10. Ash; 11. Around a lake; 12. Overhang, belt, ridge, scar, summit; 13. Winter, February; 14. 'Mother, any distance', The mother; 15. Church-Town; 16. Porphyria; 17. 'Before You Were Mine', 'Marilyn' (5) Monroe; 18. 'eighteen years ago' (1); 19. 'Neutral Tones'; 20. A hare, a mouse and a leveret, She is timid and afraid of men.

Section Two: Check your understanding

Task 1:

- Browning does not change the pace or create a build up of tension to the murder, so the reader is unprepared for what is about to happen.
- We can assume Browning does not only wish to create shock, but to highlight the chilling nature of the act and the lack of emotion in the speaker's voice as he commits the murder. Another effect is that we immediately question the sanity of the speaker.
- The speaker's attitude before the murder suggests a possessive nature in which he wishes Porphyria to 'give herself to [him] for ever' (25), but there is no suggestion that he has murderous intent.

Task 2:

- The poem is written in six quatrains, which all have a regular, repetitive pattern that is written in iambic tetrameter. The regular full rhyme and half-rhyme also help to push the rhythm along.
- The effect of these repetitive techniques working together is that they seem to mimic the regular rhythm of a plough, 'Dipping and rising' (16).
- Heaney also uses enjambment so that one line runs into another. In the image 'with a single pluck/ Of reins' (8, 9) it runs from one verse to another. This makes the reader feel as if they are turning with the plough to come back down the field again.

PART THREE, page 70

Section One: Check your knowledge

1. 'Eden Rock'; 2.'When We Two Parted', 'Love's Philosophy'; 3. 'Letters from Yorkshire'; 4. Porphyria's Lover'; 5. Family ties, or mother/son relationship; 6. 'Walking Away', 'letting go' is the theme of separation; 7. 'Sonnet 29 – "I think of thee!"'; 8. 'Before You Were Mine', 'Singh Song!'; 11. Victorian period; 10. Family love, romantic love, passionate love, true love, illicit love, perverse love, desire, close friendship, reconciliation.

Section Two: Check your understanding

Task:

- In verse three when the young wife runs away, the farmer and a group of people (presumably men) pursue her. Apparently she has no choice about staying with her husband or leaving him.
- When the wife is caught she is taken home where they 'turned the key upon her, fast' (19). During the Victorian period, husbands were legally allowed to confine their wives.
- The farmer describes the wife's attempts at escape, in a tone of mild disbelief. There is no understanding of the wife's position, even though she is 'All in a shiver and a scare' (17). He does not question his rights of ownership over her.

PART FOUR, page 83

Section One: Check your knowledge

1. A mountain represents the grandfather; 2. The farmer in 'The Farmer's Bride'; 3. Sestet; 4. 'Follower', The image refers to the ploughman's/father's shoulders; 5. Iambic pentameter; 6. It creates a pause in a line of poetry; 7. 'skirted', 'silent', 'Winter Swans'; 8. Within a line of poetry; 9. The recurring rise and fall in the rhythms of speech/poetry; 10. 'Neutral Tones', 'God-curst sun' represents love that deceives in a failed relationship.

Section Two: Check your understanding

Task:

- Owen Sheers uses the metaphor of the swans to convey the theme of renewal. The swans arrive together and remain together on the lake, contrasting with the estranged couple.

- Images such as 'with a show of tipping in unison' (8) have the effect of evoking togetherness while 'like boats righting in rough weather' (12) suggest resolving difficulties together.

- The metaphor also affects the speaker and his partner, who renew their relationship by following the swans' example.

MARK SCHEME

PRACTICE TASK 1, pages 94–5

Question 1 – 'An Irish Airman Foresees His Death'

Points you could have made:

- the poet uses key images to present the speaker's feelings about war (e.g. war's pointlessness: 'a waste of breath'; its nationalism: 'public men' and 'cheering crowds')
- the poet uses key images to present the speaker's feelings about the impact of war on himself (e.g. sense of foreboding: the poem's title; disconnection with normal life: 'above the clouds'; rational, clear thinking: 'balanced all'; feels no sense of duty :'nor duty bade me fight')
- the nouns, 'tumult' (chaos of war) and 'impulse' (speaker's desire) are the only words that suggest passionate feeling. However both are associated with the adjective 'lonely', suggesting a single instance/exception
- the repetitive metre (iambic tetrameter) combined with the regular rhyme scheme and full end rhyme have the effect of reinforcing certainty about the speaker's fate
- the voice (first person) speaks directly to the reader without shifting who it addresses, reinforcing the sense of conviction that the words are 'true'
- the monologue form is not divided into quatrains. It is delivered directly and consistently to the reader, reinforcing certainty.

Question 2 – Comparison points

Points you could have made:

You could have identified similarities between the two poems:

- both poets present the idea that war is outside the control of those who are called to fight, whether people or animals. (e.g. 'An Irish Airman Foresees His Death': 'I shall meet my fate'; 'Horses Aboard': 'wondering why')
- both poets present a picture of war that is unaffected by images of glory or patriotic sentiment (e.g. 'An Irish Airman Foresees His Death': 'No likely end could bring them loss'; 'Horses Aboard': '"war-waste" classed')

PRACTICE TASK 2, pages 96–7

Question 1 – 'I Remember, I Remember'

Points you could have made:

- the strongly personal first person voice reflects on the past ('the house where I was born') and contrasts childhood joy with current sadness – even wishing, it seems, for death in the last two lines of the first verse.
- the repetition of 'remember' from the start, and as the first line of each stanza, focuses the reader's attention on a range of childhood memories. Then, in each verse these past memories are juxtaposed with the present through the use of tense forms ('where I *was* born' and 'I often *wish*') and comparatives such as 'now', 'than' and 'yet', all indicating a change of view.
- the poet's use of sound is also notable in the regular rhymes (2nd and 4th; 6th and 8th lines) which are broken up by unrhymed pairs of lines to undercut the sing-song nature of the verse, matching the bitter-sweet mood.
- the poet presents positive images of the past: the sun personified as a friendly visitor ('peeping in'); the colourful roses; the 'light' lilies indicating youth and life; and by implication a different sort of 'lightness' as alluded to by 'my spirit flew in feathers', suggesting the airy freedom of birds contrasted with the burden of age – 'that is so heavy now.'

- also, ideas related to childish innocence and joy – the childish swing where the speaker compared himself to a swallow; the belief that the 'tree-tops' were almost touching the sky – are brought to an abrupt end by the weight of experience, suggesting that the speaker has not lived life as he should have done, and is now 'farther off from Heaven' than when a child.

Question 2 – Comparison points

Points you could have made:

- both poems deal with the idea of childhood being a place of joy and comfort, and how readily these ideas can be brought to mind: Lawrence's ideas are evoked by the immediate experience of hearing a woman sing, but Hood's are ongoing memories.
- Lawrence explores the idea of how children relate to the adult world, focusing in on vivid, physical detail through the senses – the 'boom of the tingling strings' of a piano, the 'pressing' of the 'small, poised feet' of his mother – so that the speaker's past life is brought more sharply into focus. Hood's evocation of childhood shows how the natural world creates lasting impressions – sun, flowers, robin, swallows, fir-trees.
- Hood suggests childhood is untroubled and regrets the loss of innocence. It represents a sort of perfection, which conjures up spiritual ideas about a lost Eden. Lawrence's vision of childhood is more homely in its description of the 'cosy parlour', though it too is perfect in a different way – having a sort of 'glamour'. He perhaps implies his idea of childhood may be rose-tinted and that the poem is more a comment on the power of music to stir emotion – almost wickedly – hence the use of words like 'insidious' and 'betrays', as it is about a desire to be a child again.

PRACTICE TASK 3, page 110

Points you could have made:

- discussion of the main theme of parental love and related theme of separation in 'Walking Away'
- how the language reflects the theme of separation (e.g. the repetition of 'away'; the powerful simile 'like a satellite/Wrenched from its orbit') and the effects they create
- the depiction of the child's vulnerability in the nature imagery and how its effects highlight the poignancy of the parting
- how the themes are mirrored in the slow rhythm of the poem and the effect of enjambment
- how the structure of the poem is partly shaped by the speaker's shift in mood at the end of the poem; how he understands the memory's meaning, which is summed up in the last two lines
- discussion of a range of similarities and differences and their effects in 'Walking Away' and the other poem of your choice.

GENERAL SKILLS

Make a judgement about your level based on the points you made (above) and the skills you showed.

Level	Key elements	Writing skills	Tick your level
Very high	**Very well-structured answer which gives a rounded and convincing viewpoint.** You use very detailed analysis of the poets' methods and effects on the reader, using precise references which are fluently woven into what you say. You draw inferences, consider more than one perspective or angle, including the context where relevant, and make interpretations about the poems as a whole.	You spell and punctuate with consistent accuracy, and use a very wide range of vocabulary and sentence structures to achieve effective control of meaning.	
Good to High	**A thoughtful, detailed response with well-chosen references.** At the top end, you address all aspects of the task in a clearly expressed way, and examine key aspects and poetic techniques in detail. You are beginning to consider implications, explore alternative interpretations or ideas; you do this fairly regularly and with some confidence.	You spell and punctuate with considerable accuracy, and use a considerable range of vocabulary and sentence structures to achieve general control of meaning.	
Mid	**A consistent response with clear understanding of the main ideas shown.** You use a range of references to support your ideas and your viewpoint is logical and easy to follow. Some evidence of commenting on writers' effects and poetic techniques, though more needed.	You spell and punctuate with reasonable accuracy, and use a reasonable range of vocabulary and sentence structures.	
Lower	**Some relevant ideas but an inconsistent and rather simple response in places.** You show you have understood the task and you make some points to support what you say, but the evidence is not always well chosen. Your analysis is a bit basic and you do not comment in much detail on the poets' methods.	Your spelling and punctuation is inconsistent and your vocabulary and sentence structures are both limited. Some of these make your meaning unclear.	